Grandma Wears Hiking Boots

A personal guide
to the
Okanagan Valley

Laurie Carter

Little White Publishing

Grandma Wears Hiking Boots: A personal guide to the Okanagan Valley
Copyright © 2010 by Laurie Carter

Little White Publishing
2-2095 Boucherie Road
Westbank BC Canada V4T 1Z4
www.littlewhitepublishing.com

Library and Archives Canada Cataloguing in Publication
Carter, Laurie
Grandma wears hiking boots : a personal guide to the Okanagan Valley / Laurie Carter.

ISBN 978-0-9812451-0-2

1. Carter, Laurie--Travel--British Columbia--Okanagan Valley (Region).
2. Okanagan Valley (B.C. : Region)--Description and travel.
3. Trails--British Columbia--Okanagan Valley (Region)--Guidebooks.
4. Okanagan Valley (B.C. : Region)--Guidebooks. I. Title.

GV199.44.C22B7412 2010   796.5109711'5   C2010-904658-7

Printed and bound in Canada by Friesens

Cover and interior design by Mishell Raedeke
Cover original photos by Laurie Carter, Bruce Kemp
Cover composite photo by Mishell Raedeke
Maps by James White
Photos by Laurie Carter unless otherwise credited

For

Barbara Eckersley White

whose example taught me love,
the value of family,
and the need to find whatever joy we can
in the present moment,
for that may be all we have.

Thank you, Mom

Contents

OKANAGAN VALLEY
N
To Kamloops
To Sicamous
Enderby
97A
97
Mabel Lake
O'Keefe Ranch
Armstrong
Silver Star Mtn
Swan Lake
Vernon
To Nakusp
6
Fintry Provincial Park
Kalamalka Lake
Wood Lake
Bear Creek Provincial Park
Duck Lake
Lake
West Kelowna
Kelowna
Crystal Mtn
Big White
To Merritt
97C
Telemark
Okanagan
Peachland
Myra Canyon
KVR / Trans Canada Trail
33
97
Chute Lake
Summerland
Naramata
Penticton
Skaha Lake
Apex Mtn
Kaleden
Beaverdell
Okanagan Falls
To Hope
Vaseux Lake
3A
3
Oliver
Keremeos
Okanagan R
Mt Baldy
To Midway
Mt Kobau
3A
Cathedral Provincial Park
Osoyoos
Rock Creek
Canada
USA
Osoyoos Lake
Sketch not to scale nor meant for accurate travel planning.

Introduction

DRAGGED KICKING AND SCREAMING!

That's how I landed in the Okanagan Valley. I'd just moved into my dream home, an 1850s red brick farmhouse originally built as a tavern and inn on a busy stagecoach route in Ontario's Niagara Peninsula. You can imagine my dismay when I learned my then husband's business was bringing us to what I regarded as the "Wet Coast" —to a valley I vaguely remembered from elementary school as a fruit growing region, where the oldest building was apparently a log cabin constructed by the first European to settle here, several years *after* my Ontario idyll began welcoming guests in a thriving colonial community. I was not happy.

We arrived on a Saturday.

By Tuesday I was a born again Okanaganite.

True, my new home was only twenty years old and built of cedar, but when I looked out the window, virtually any window in the house, I beheld a panorama from north of Knox Mountain to the southern reaches of Kelowna, with a bonus glimpse of snow-capped Big White on the horizon. I was captivated, mesmerized. It's a miracle I ever finished unpacking. I would just stand and stare.

When I stepped outside, it felt like camping, the air heavy with the scent of the ponderosa pine and Douglas fir forest that surrounded our yard. Walk in any direction and I was hiking. Stand still and I might spot a deer or even a black bear. The spirit moved me, and like so many converts, I became a zealot.

At first my quest to learn about the valley was pretty much random. But the move from Ontario forced on me not only a change in venue, but also a change in career. And as my corporate life receded into memory, the demands of a new writing life coincided with this new passion. Spurred by the need to produce fresh stories for a weekly travel column,

I became even more devoted to learning about the people and places in my new home. Early on it occurred to me that my collected experiences and observations might make a useful guide for others interested in touring or just learning a little more about the Okanagan.

Grandma Wears Hiking Boots is the result.

As you read you'll come to know two other characters, both central players in my valley story. One is my indefatigable hiking partner, the octogenarian mountain goat, bushwhacking male parental unit who so often maps out the trails and cajoles me away from my keyboard. The other is the long-suffering and good-natured guy who shares my love of food, has taught me more than I ever expected to know about wine, and in a moment of reckless abandon, said, "I do." I poke a lot of fun at Dad and Bruce, but I hope you can feel the love.

This book is as much memoir as guidebook and it contains stories of some tours that are no longer offered while others show the evolution of particular attractions over a number of years. This is my very personal guide to the Okanagan. I don't apologize to readers who visit a place or hike a trail or sample a restaurant and find their experience different from mine. I've written about what the Okanagan is like for me.

But I'm also very much interested in what it's like for you. I invite you to visit my website, follow my blog, write in your comments and share your own stories.

Looking forward to hearing from you at www.LaurieCarter.com.

Laurie Carter
Westbank, BC
June 2010

I take baby Alex on his first hike to Hardy Falls. Facing page: Hardy Falls trail.

Chapter 1

Grandma's Favourite Hikes

I WAS A SERIOUS COUCH POTATO, and darn proud of it.
By the close of my fourth decade on life's trail I'd turned my back on the
habits of a very athletic youth. My only concession to physical activity
was a few weekends of skiing each year, agreed to very reluctantly
as a family activity to get us outdoors in winter. How I longed for
a warm fire and my soft sofa. Then we moved to the Okanagan.
More precisely, we moved to the bush in the Okanagan. Just 15
minutes from downtown Kelowna, my home was surrounded
by ponderosa pines and Douglas firs. Bears wandered through
my yard and mule deer were a regular sight as I drove into town.
When I stepped out my back door, I was on a hiking trail.
Suddenly that couch didn't look so appealing. And while I make a
lot of jokes in this chapter about the immutable fact that every trail
in BC goes up, my only regret is that I have to spend too much time
tapping away at a keyboard instead of lacing up my hiking boots.

Hardy Falls

IT'S A BALMY FALL SUNDAY. I've been buried in the office cave all week and I *need* a hit of nature—something in a waterfall and maybe a bit of light salmon spotting. Not a really tough trick in the Okanagan, unless your hiking partner is a twenty-three-pound six-month-old. You try pushing a stroller up the switchbacks to see the falls in Bear Creek Provincial Park. Sure this grandma wears hiking boots, but get serious.

Ditto for the eight-hundred-gazillion steps to the platform overlooking the falls at Fintry Provincial Park. Mission Creek Greenway in Kelowna is pretty and pushable, plus it's equipped with spawning kokanee salmon at this time of year, but alas, no waterfall.

If you're hoping there's a punch line coming, here it is—Hardy Falls.

This pocket park, named for Harry Hardy, one of the area's first

Hardy Falls, Peachland.

At a Glance

Hardy Falls Regional Park straddles Deep Creek (shown on topo maps as Peachland Creek). Parking is available on Hardy Road off Hwy 97 just south of Peachland. It's an easy 15-minute walk to the falls. Directly across Hwy 97 (on the lakeshore) is Antlers Beach Regional Park.

orchardists, is easy-access, easy-push—and promises both waterfalls and hormonal fish.

Alex grins and drools as his stroller bumps along the path under a canopy of golden cottonwoods, crossing and recrossing Deep Creek via a series of clompy wooden bridges. The air is as moist and soft as a facial mist, although it comes up short in the aromatherapy department. The earthy scent is nice, the hint of stale cat food, not so much. But what can you do. Those poor salmon—so much work, then belly up on the beach. And only the very strongest make it all the way to my favourite spot, the pool below the falls (since altered by a landslide).

I park the stroller in a cul-de-sac formed by the sheer-sided canyon walls. In autumn the cascade of water is a thin echo of the roaring spring runoff, but still mesmerizing. At this time of year, the reduced flow makes it easy to discern changing patterns in the falling water. It's a different experience from the sheer volume and power of the early spring show.

We gaze into the clear water as the brilliant red kokanee manoeuvre to complete their life cycle. Well, I watch the fish. Alex is pretty much occupied with fist chewing. But he seems to enjoy himself and I know I feel better.

Golden Mile Trail

IT'S ALL ABOUT MOTIVATION. Never mind the thermometer-popping temperature (think eggs frying on sidewalks). Ignore the potentially life-threatening fact that finger-tapping a keyboard is my most strenuous regular exercise. The promise of a Tinhorn Creek wine tasting at the end of the trail has me lacing up my boots and heading for the hills—well, that and a looming deadline. (Now we're talking motivation.)

I've done my homework. As per web search instructions I collect a trail guide at the tourism info centre in the town of Oliver and drive south to the winery parking lot where a kiosk displays an overview map of the ten-kilometre hike plus an optional side trail to stone ruins left from 19th century gold mining days.

Right, I hear you. If I'm already at the winery, why not just get on with the tasting and motor home in air-conditioned comfort? Believe me, if I thought I could get a seventy-five-word feature past my editor, I'd do it. But he's so prickly that way. I start walking.

The first section is a steep downhill and hard left turn onto a country road. It's steamy walking the pavement between the orchards with sprinklers misting the leaves and ripening fruit—voluptuous peaches, red and green apples, russet pears, deep violet-blue grapes. Conventional trees, tall, round and leafy; spindly dwarfs tethered to wires

At a Glance

The Golden Mile Trail is a ten-kilometre loop with the main trailhead at Tinhorn Creek Vineyards (www.tinhorn.com) in Oliver. It includes stretches on public roads, through orchards and vineyards, and a grassland and forest hiking trail with excellent valley views. A short side trail near the winery leads to stamp mill ruins left from gold mining days. Visit the ruins as a side trip on the ten-kilometre hike or via a two-kilometre loop from the winery. For an easier hike that takes in the best views, try the 6.8-kilometre round-trip between the Old Fairview Road access point and the stamp mill ruins. There is a trail map kiosk at Tinhorn Creek and trail maps are available at the Oliver Visitor Centre. Use some judgement with this trail guide and pair it up with a local map since the directions and road signs don't always match and some trail signs appear to be missing.

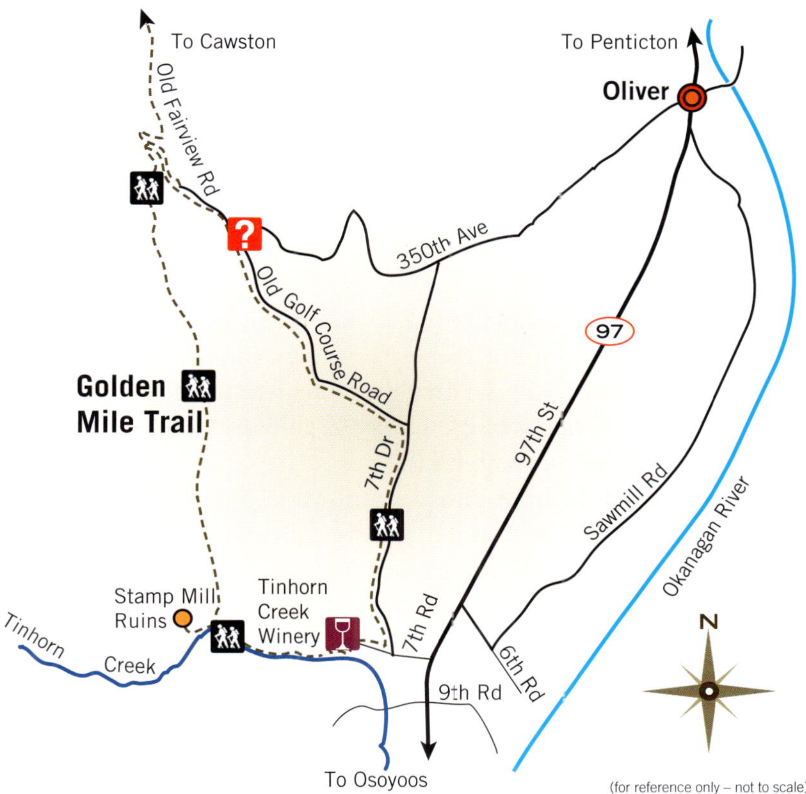

with arterial irrigation lines running down the rows; apple crates piled at the ready; my glasses smudge as I press the camera against my sweaty face.

The next junction turns west toward Fairview Mountain Golf Club. As I begin the uphill grade an apple-balm breeze spills through gaps in the trees (thank you) and dries my face. The incline increases, the orchards disappear, but aspens and ponderosa pines cast pools of shade. The hills beyond are brown with tinder dry grass and rabbit brush is just starting its yellow bloom. A bird cannon cracks in the distance.

At the edge of a large clearing I'm intrigued by two stone plinths standing alone among the weeds flanking a gravel pathway that curves toward a rustic bench in the middle of nowhere. Presumably I've found downtown Fairview. I guzzle water and try to imagine this empty meadow as the largest settlement in the South Okanagan.

The only evidence that the town ever existed is an iron cross marking the location of a church (later moved to Okanagan Falls) and an information kiosk. Yet little more than a century ago this dry grass field was home to over five hundred souls.

Gold was discovered here in 1887 and a string of mines followed. A decade later, plans were laid out for a town. Soon there were stores, offices, churches—and in 1899, the "finest hostelry in the Interior" opened. Known as the Big Teepee for the pyramidal roof on its corner tower, the three-storey Fairview Hotel was a bellwether for the town's fortunes. When it burned in 1902, gold prices were falling and the owners decided not to rebuild.

Fairview faded into a ghost town. Most of its buildings were shipped down the hill as the new community of Oliver started to grow in the 1920s. Now, even the ghosts seem to have moved on. But the view that gave the town its name, from Osoyoos Lake to Oliver, with Mount Baldy towering beyond the valley, is still remarkably fair.

Further *up* the road (I'm starting to harbour murderous thoughts about that editor), where a cattle guard divides pavement from gravel, I notice the first trail sign I've seen since leaving the winery. The creek to the left is a bare trickle hidden in the trees, but the water's clear and cold. I splash every bit of exposed flesh—surprised that no hiss or puff of steam erupts where it hits.

Aspens and alders crowd the riparian creek zone, while across the road, spaced ponderosas hold the steep dry bank. Something big rustles the thick brush and I shade my eyes against the high beam sunlight streaming through the branches. Nothing. But I know a big animal is close. I move cautiously on. A couple of cars pass, raising rooster tails of dust. *Up* and *up*. My calves shriek abuse. Near a string of wild rose bushes, red hips picked nearly clean, a neat pile of scat—black and fresh—confirms my suspicion that I'm not alone. I tell myself the bear has tastier options than a sweaty hiker—but move along smartly all the same.

Soon after, the single dirt track that loops back to the winery forks left into the forest. The baking air smells of dusty pine—venerable giants not yet ravaged by rampaging beetles. A few hundred metres along, a splash of red in the undergrowth snags my attention and I realize that it's a sleeping bag splayed open and abandoned in the dirt. *What about that bear?* I move on—*very* smartly.

But the heat and quiet and steady rhythm soon calm me. Bill Bryson (*A Walk in the Woods*) is right about the therapy of walking—eventually you think of little but putting one foot in front of the other. And the only wildlife that takes any interest is a bumblebee that buzzes in for a look at my yellow shirt and, disappointed at not finding a sunflower, zooms on. Switchbacks carry me up and up (notice the recurring theme) until I top a final rise and, snap, the valley reappears. The track suddenly leaves the sheltering trees and I'm on the grasslands. It's easy going, cruising the relative flat, and I have company all the time with grasshoppers flitting across the path, yellow butterflies chasing each other from leaf to stem and

Water break stop and self-portrait at Fairview townsite on the Golden Mile Trail.

small birds cheep-eeping from the ground and the branches of the widely spaced pines.

I'm so strongly reminded of a game walk I took in South Africa that I wouldn't be shocked to see a rhino foraging on the far side of the valley or the head of a giraffe rising above a clump of aspens.

The trail starts to climb again, up into the pine forest—perfect deer country. I keep looking but don't expect to see any. They'll be bedded down for the day (no pushy editors). My pace has slowed, but at least there's shade. Finally I reach the small signpost announcing the side path to a stamp mill that once functioned as part of the local gold mining operations. I am sorely tempted to take a pass, but you-know-who will want pics.

The stone ruins stand in a leafy clearing partly obscured by alders and sumac. I check a convenient boulder for sunning rattlers (all I need now is a butt-bite) and collapse. Between my slowly shallowing breaths and the occasional chirp from a high branch, the silence is complete. I'm thinking that it's a beautiful place to recharge your batteries, maybe bring a picnic. I can even spare a kind thought for that editor—until I push off and hit the toe-crunching, knee-screaming, rocky, goat track down the mountain—just cruel at the end of the trail. But I focus on the reward.

Manhandling the huge wooden winery door, I step into a pool of silken cool and after a brief submariner's shower in the ladies, approached the tasting bar smelling marginally better than an old sneaker. One sip of the Pinot Gris (smooth, luscious), half a glass of water (to cleanse my palate), a sip of Gewurz (big, fruity)—and I'm ready to keel over.

"Just finished the hike and this is going straight to my head," I explain to the attendant, who nods sympathetically. "I'll just skip the tasting and buy."

She beams and starts piling bottles into a divided case. "Would you like me to carry this out for you." (My purple-red cheeks must have alarmed her.) A semblance of pride asserts itself and I decline, staggering as she sets the box in my arms. Somehow I reach the car. It's all about motivation.

Glen Canyon Regional Park

THE HIKING PARTNER FROM HELL (an octogenarian who delights in walking me into the ground) keeps badgering me to check out this park. Dad knows I'm always looking for new trails to write about and he promises this one holds a couple of surprises.

Glen Canyon is a linear park, straddling several kilometres of Powers Creek as it makes its last dash to Okanagan Lake near the Westbank town centre of West Kelowna. Named for early English settler, William "Billy" Powers, the creek provided First Nations people with water, vegetation and wildlife and it became a central feature for development after European settlement began.

The full trail system isn't yet complete with private land and Highway 97 blocking access in a few places. But there are entry points in the Glenrosa area north of the highway and off Gellatly Road to the south. We start on the lowest section.

It's really silly that I haven't hiked it before with the trailhead only a couple of kilometres from my back door. The path starts near a spot in the creek where a fish ladder is laid out for spawning kokanee salmon. At first we walk through a leafy riparian zone (delicious relief in mid-summer) with thick stands of scouring rush, a plant that looks to me like anorexic bamboo. Along a short side trail to the water's edge, Dad shows me a fish counting box fitted into the channel above a small dam. Immediately upstream, the creek disappears into a narrow gorge.

At a Glance

Glen Canyon is a seventy-four hectare linear park west of the Westbank town centre in West Kelowna. It follows the flow of Powers Creek into Okanagan Lake. The trail is not yet continuous, so respect private property. For more details click on Regional Parks at www.regionaldistrict.com. North of Hwy 97, take Glenrosa Road for access points at Blue Jay Road (off McGinnes Road) and Aberdeen Road (off Webber Road). South of the highway, access from Gellatly Road at the mailboxes and at the fish ladders near Whitworth Road. A trailhead map is posted on the info kiosk at the Aberdeen Road entrance.

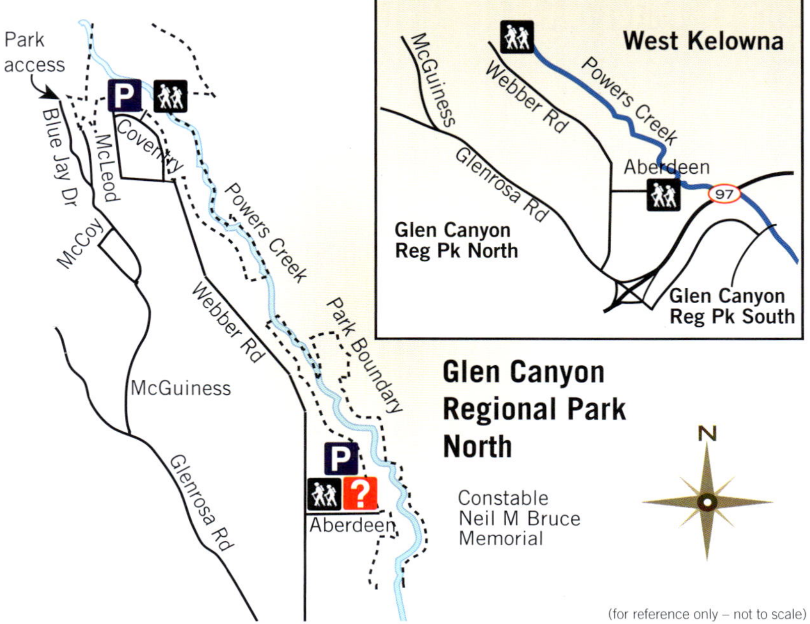

Naturally our path is up and over (always with the climbing in this country). Thankfully, wooden steps have been installed to make it easier and safer. From this point on, it's like working an outdoor Stairmaster—up out of the canyon to sunny, dry ponderosa studded hillsides where the air smells dusty and lookouts provide glimpses of a shimmering silver ribbon amid the crowding dark trees below— then down into the canyon, the temperature dropping as the roar of rushing water grows louder and louder.

Strategically placed benches on the stairways (thank you!) give me a place to sit and catch my breath. I'd like to hang around and veg for awhile, this is such an amazing little hideaway right in the heart of town, but the old goat (consider this a descriptive not a pejorative) just won't slow down.

Up in the sunshine, I spot a lavender-coloured mariposa lily, just at the end of its prime and nibbled around the edges. Mariposas are a pretty rare site, but I can see from the number of plants in the area that a week ago, there would have been lots of blossoms here. Down in the shady patches, the white flowers of mock orange are also in

Hummingbird chicks in a trailside nest.

Remnants of a wooden water flume rotting beside the Flume Trail in Glen Canyon Regional Park.

decline, but still pretty, and berries are just starting to come on—blue Oregon grape and something brownish, I don't know what.

This isn't a long hike. It takes us forty minutes, including photo stops (some of which I admit have more to do with catching my breath in the wake of Mr. Super-hiker than any particular Kodak moment). Lots to see, great exercise—excellent quickie getaway.

But he isn't through humiliating me. As fast as we can jump in the car and motor up to the Glenrosa area on the north side of Highway 97 (barely enough time to get the AC pumping), we're shrugging back into our daypacks. We enter Glen Canyon from a neighbourhood playground, Last Mountain Park. The access is a relatively steep switchback path through widely spaced ponderosa pines and Douglas firs down into the canyon. It joins the Creekside Trail (rated moderate on a map we find later at an info kiosk), one of four interconnected trails in this section of the park.

Along Powers Creek with its multiple rapids and mini-waterfalls, the vegetation grows thicker and includes Solomon's seal, honeysuckle, blue clematis and horsetails along with Douglas maple shrub, aspen, mock orange, dogwood, Oregon grape, thimbleberries and falsebox. Where we first join the trail, the mock orange is getting a little shaggy, but farther north (and higher up), in a different microclimate, it's in full bloom. Don't get the idea that I'm any kind of plant guru. Apart from the mock orange and Oregon grape, I'd be at a loss, but Dad recognizes some and I pick up the rest from an interpretive sign at the info kiosk.

At a point on the trail across the creek from West Kelowna's new pump house, Dad stops and points uphill. It's like that with him— always up. But I forgive him (silently, there's no breath for talking) when we connect with the Flume Trail. Not only is it rated easy, but this path shows off a real bit of Okanagan history.

The first remnant I see of the Westbank Water Users Group aqueduct is a section of wooden flume, weathered grey boards deeply grooved like a wrinkled old face and bearded with wisps of green lichen, stray planks rotted out and fallen to the ground beneath. We walk the path parallel to the old waterway a short distance until it connects with a deep mossy-green concrete trough snaking through the forest at an almost imperceptible incline. My partner (an engineer by training who, despite my ribbing over his killer pace, adds immeasurably to these hikes with his mini-lectures—*and don't ever tell him I said so*) explains that the wooden sections were used in terrain where building the more durable concrete flumes was too expensive.

I try to picture what it must have been like to survey the best route to keep a moderate grade, then pack all the building materials on horseback into the deep canyon. It really was an incredible feat and absolutely essential to the development of agriculture in the region.

We turn back at the point we reckon the flume must have come off the creek (there's no clear evidence of the exact spot), although we could have kept going. If I weren't nearing collapse, we could carry on along the moderate Black Canyon Trail, which was cut by a forestry recreation crew in 1992 through Black Canyon to Lambly Lake (known locally as Bear Lake).

Hikers who just want to see the old aqueducts can access the Flume Trail via Blue Jay Drive. I mentally questioned why we, too, didn't take this easy route—but then we'd have missed the canyon floor. And on the way out, we wouldn't have met the woman walking her dog who tells us about a tiny hummingbird nest that she checks daily. On a branch right above the well-travelled trail, it hangs completely undisturbed and inhabited by two sleeping chicks. Definitely worth the huffing and puffing.

Back at the car, Super-hiker decides we should look for the other access points to the park and we drive around until we find the Aberdeen Road entrance where the interpretive kiosk gives me those details on flora and fauna. It's also the site of a stone memorial marking the heroism of Constable Neil Bruce, an RCMP officer who was fatally wounded in April 1965 while attempting to rescue a young woman who was being sexually assaulted in a cabin beside the creek. The stone is simple and very moving.

Bear Creek Trails

WHEN I WANT TO GIVE VISITORS the full-meal-deal Okanagan nature experience in a compact morning hike, Bear Creek Provincial Park is my go-to place. It's easy access, right on Westside Road directly across Okanagan Lake from Kelowna, with trail options that show off all the attractions from cottonwood riparian zone to arid ponderosa pine parkland with a waterfall thrown in for bonus points.

The easy Loop Trail is ideal for infirm elderly relatives (more on this later)—or complete couch potatoes who aren't up to the ninety-metre elevation change (repeated a couple of times to make sure you notice) of the Canyon Rim and Mid-Canyon trails. It stays at low elevation in the shade of the cottonwood trees, major relief on scorching July/August days, crossing and recrossing Bear Creek on hefty timber bridges.

It's also a great little hike for kids in late-September to early-October when the loop is especially cool, and I'm not just talking temperature here. The bridges make ideal platforms for shameless voyeurism, spying on kokanee salmon as they struggle upstream to spawn. It can get a little ripe with fish corpses littering the banks, since these poor guys die at the end of their journey, but we like to think they pass on smiling. And the creekside buffet makes a lot of black bears very happy as they bulk up for winter. Warning signs are posted, although it's rare to spot one during the day. They're not much interested in tangling with people. Still, caution is always wise (unless the kids are acting up and you're tempted to offer the bears a little change of diet).

At a Glance

A large trailhead map (available online for download from the BC Parks website at www.env.gov.bc.ca/bcparks) shows the course of the stream that everybody calls Bear Creek, although its official name is Lambly Creek. (Some maps show both names, some choose one or the other.) Three trail options include a short loop; the Canyon Rim trail and the Mid-Canyon trail. Both canyon trails provide views of Bear Creek Falls. Mid-Canyon connects with Canyon Rim to form a medium-length loop west of the creek. It's also aligned to give you a shortcut back to the parking lot if your legs give out on the rim.

Personally, I don't spend much time on the loop. Canyon Rim is my trail and spring is my favourite time for hiking it. Summer days get so hot you really need to stick to early morning or evening unless you're into serious self-abuse. But in spring it's good pretty much any time of day. Snowmelt in the high country puts maximum flow over the waterfall and this is the best season for wildflowers.

Saskatoon bushes arch over the trail in bridal bowers of feathery white, the shiny green and red-tinged leaves of Oregon grape cradle tight clusters of yellow blossoms and arrowleaf balsamroot sprouts in profusion. Found only in BC's Okanagan Valley and the Okanogan region of Washington State, balsamroot is Kelowna's official flower. The sturdy plants with their arrow-shaped leaves gather in clumps of three or four or a dozen daisy-like blooms. They manage to thrive on sandy and stony hillsides and love the open ground beneath ponderosa pines and Douglas firs. Great splashes of sunny yellow on the spring-green landscape, they soak up the moisture left over from winter before the hills are baked to golden brown.

Staircases along the trail protect delicate vegetation and make the going easier for hikers in Bear Creek Provincial Park.

A series of lookouts provide different perspectives on Bear Creek Canyon and Bear Creek Falls.

I enlist a couple of companions for my end-of-April pilgrimage. Bruce, my equally out-of-shape husband, shares my shame as my eighty-something sire (extremely fit elderly relative) shows only minor impatience at our complete inability to keep up. The Saskatoons and balsamroot are prime and I have no qualms in blaming our slow progress up the path and stairways (erected to reduce erosion and wear on the steepest sections) on our frequent photo stops. Nothing to do with lack of conditioning—although I have to admit that I feel like a biathlete, mentally willing my beached-whale breathing to slow enough for me to get off a shot at something under a thousandth of a second at ISO 800. (For you point-and-shooters, we're talking major camera shake).

Fortunately the views provide another legitimate excuse for breathers. As we climb higher, Okanagan Lake opens out behind us and we can see more and more of Kelowna on the far side. In the foreground, Sunday sailors race for the windward mark and overhead a hawk sails in lazy circles on the gathering thermals. It's overcast, not much good for scenic panoramas, so I start looking sideways at the cutbanks and down at my feet. Snowflake-sized blossoms on hair stems are so tiny I ask Bruce to put his finger in the frame for scale.

The first lookout gives the best view of Bear Creek Falls. Brimful from the runoff, white water crowds through the narrow gorge, surging toward the lake. At the second lookout, dear old Dad waits patiently until we catch up then launches into a geology lesson. I follow his pointing finger along the curves of rock on the opposite wall of the deep, narrow canyon where millennia ago, layers of lava flowed over a bed of even more ancient sediment.

Mercifully the trail eventually takes a downhill turn and another stairway makes it easy going to the creek crossing. If you look up at the canyon wall on the north side you can see a few segments of columnar basalt. And this day, a lone clump of balsamroot beside the bridge stands in vivid yellow contrast against the white water of the swollen creek. Bruce and I loiter side-by-side on the bridge, staring into the rushing water, engulfed in the sound volleyed back and forth between rock walls, our nostrils filled with the smell of earth and damp.

Respite too short. When you live in the mountains you soon learn the corollary of Newton's Law—what goes down, must go up. This trail proves the rule.

Some way along we reconnect with our phantom hiking buddy who's scouting ahead to find one of the geocaches stashed in the park. Bruce takes one look at the proposed off-trail route, drops his pack and settles firmly on a convenient stump. I on the other hand am suicidally determined to follow where the parental unit has gone before and detour onto the scree slope. Clinging to scraggly branches to keep my balance among the shark-tooth rocks (not easy, with one hand cradling a precious camera), I struggle to keep up with the two-legged mountain goat who is retracing his steps to guide me to the cache for a photo op. Terminal show-off!

Miraculously unscathed, we rejoin Bruce and the main trail, which eventually levels off and swings out to the face of the ridge, where a strategically placed bench delivers a stunning view of the William R. Bennett Bridge and fishermen casting their lines around the edge of a log boom tethered to the shore below. I sit. Bruce (all nicely rested) and the old goat can sprint the last downhill stretch if they want. As far as I'm concerned, this is the whole point of the Canyon Rim trail. And they won't get far without me. I have the car keys.

The trailhead sign suggests two hours for this hike. I take three—no apology.

I check out the geocache Dad tracked down in Bear Creek Provincial Park.

Mission Creek Greenway

BRUCE AND I LIVED FOR A TIME in a downtown Kelowna apartment and rarely a week passed between early spring and late autumn that we didn't climb on our bikes to pedal the Mission Creek Greenway. We'd scoot along the bicycle lane on Springfield Road to the entrance of Mission Creek Regional Park and dismount at the kokanee spawning channel. As we walked our bikes across the bridge to the gravel path that parallels the creek, it was like passing through a portal to another dimension.

Unbelievable that we could remount and ride along a leafy country lane just metres from the heart of the mushrooming city. A canopy of venerable cottonwoods arches across the creek and trail like the vaulted nave of a gothic cathedral. In summer, moist air and heavy shade hold the blistering heat at bay and in the autumn, when the red-bodied salmon feel the urge to come home, slanting rays filter through the butter-yellow leaves like sunlight through stained glass windows. Keeping with the religious metaphor, this is a story of redemption. The Mission Creek Greenway is the result of visionary and dedicated community activism that has taken an environmental travesty and turned it into an ecological treasure.

About one quarter of the water that finds its way into Okanagan Lake each year runs between the banks of Mission Creek. It was known to the valley's first inhabitants as N'wha-kwi-sen (smoothing stones) and provided the spawning grounds for millions of kokanee salmon. For time untold it was the site of an important native fishery.

At a Glance

Mission Creek Regional Park is located on Springfield Road in Kelowna. Within the ninety-two hectare enclave there are twelve kilometres of hiking trails; a one-kilometre spawning channel (kokanee viewing in September and October); composting education and xeriscape gardens; and the Environmental Education Centre for the Okanagan (EEOC). For more info visit www.regionaldistrict.com. The Mission Creek Greenway runs east and west from the park—phase one toward Okanagan Lake and phase two toward Gallagher's Canyon. To learn more, visit www.greenway.kelowna.bc.ca.

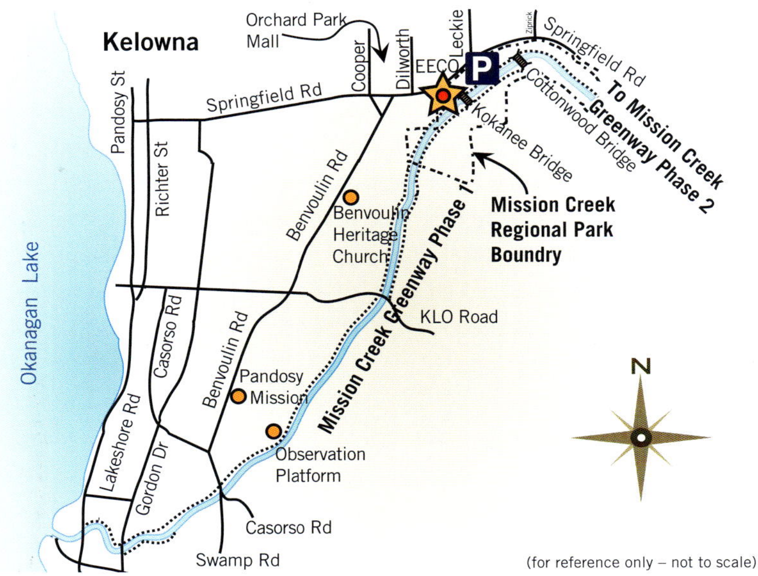

European settlement changed everything. In the 1800s, as much as $80,000 worth of gold was mined from the creek's gravel bed. Agricultural practices and burgeoning development from the 1950s onward saw the creek straightjacketed within a levee system, the waters poisoned and the spawning grounds ruined.

Sometimes, however, humankind proves that what we mess up, we can also fix. Through the efforts of determined volunteers, community fundraising (I actually "own" one metre of the Greenway) and with just enough political will, the water again runs clean, spawning kokanee swim in red shoals and thousands of city-dwellers get a much needed nature fix walking and biking the trail atop the levees. In 1997, Mission Creek was granted BC Heritage River status.

When we were regularly cycling the Greenway, only phase one of the project was complete—seven kilometres between Lakeshore Road and Mission Creek Regional Park. It's a broad, flat pathway (astonishing for this country) that's readily accessible for pretty much anyone. Phase two extends east from the park for 9.2-kilometres into Gallagher's Canyon. It's a different kind of experience with the trail generally narrower and including some steep hills and switchbacks.

The section we know so well is punctuated with lively interpretive signs that feature artwork selected from box loads of drawings submitted by District 23 school children. Not that we need signs to get close to the wildlife. Even when we don't catch a glimpse of the resident woodpeckers swooping between trees, their drum tattoo is a common sound. Ducks often keep pace with us, lazing in the current as we cruise along and once, as we stood quietly on the lookout platform east of Casorso Road, a white-tailed deer emerged from the brush on the far bank and bent to drink from the stream. Not bad for a city park.

Ziprick Road entrance to Mission Creek Greenway, Kelowna.

Observation platform overlooks Mission Creek east of Casorso Road.

Mount Kobau Forestry Lookout

I'M LOOKING FOR SPOTS—specifically a lake with spots (no chemical-, heat-, or psychologically-induced hallucinations involved).

My quest began quite innocently. I was flipping through a tourism brochure when the photo of a desert lake, its surface painted in colourful, otherworldly circles—like a preschooler's drawing or a collection of aquatic crop circles—brought me to a full stop. Could this be real, and just down the road. I had to see for myself.

The morning is vintage Okanagan August. As the sun climbs above the eastern ridges, it burns away an early haze leaving a familiar cobalt dome above the heat shimmer rising from rows of baking hills. Not far west of Osoyoos on Highway 3, I stop at a likely BC Government sign: Spotted Lake.

It provides all sorts of cool facts. For instance: the healing waters of Spotted Lake have long been used by First Nations people to soothe aches and pains. It's one of the most highly mineralized inland lakes in the world, containing significant concentrations of Epsom salts, calcium, sodium sulphates and trace minerals like silver and titanium. The spots are the result of summertime evaporation when the minerals crystallize, forming circles on the water's surface. This little body of water has remained almost unchanged since prehistoric times. All fascinating stuff—but where's the lake?

Standing at the junction of the highway and Mount Kobau Forest Service Road, I can see lots of hills and plenty of sage. But no lake. No spots.

At a Glance

The forestry lookout at the summit of Mount Kobau is readily accessible via the Kobau Lookout Forest Service Road, east of Osoyoos off Hwy 3. Look for a BC Government sign: Spotted Lake. The decently maintained twenty-kilometre gravel road is fine for two-wheel drive in summer, if you don't mind the potential for stone chips on your car. A one-kilometre hiking trail leads to the summit from the forestry rec site parking, which is also the trailhead for the five-kilometre Testalinden Trail. Check out www.mksp.ca for details on the Mount Kobau Star Party held annually in August.

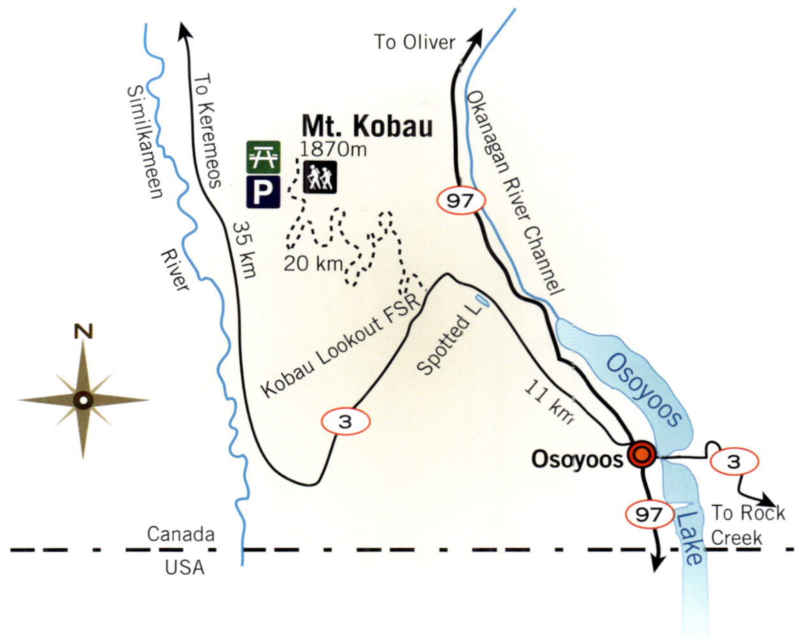

(for reference only – not to scale)

Very bizarre. I ponder the mystery, continuing to look around (the way you do when you've lost your glasses or your keys, returning time and again to places you've already checked, thinking—or not—that they might be there this time). Spotted Lake doesn't magically appear, but I do notice another sign. This one announces that it's just twenty kilometres to the Kobau fire lookout. What the heck!

Sometimes you've got to seize the moment. Temporarily abandoning my search for spots, I choose the road less travelled and in so doing discover, well, another spot.

The fire spotting station atop Mount Kobau was a square white clapboard structure that was erected in 1951. Sturdy guy wires, anchored to the exposed rock, kept it from blowing away like Dorothy's house in Kansas. This morning, standing on a wooden platform out front are a tripod-mounted scope and a gray-bearded, pony-tailed man with a thick-coated husky dog stretched out at his feet.

The man is Ken Bushey, a ten-year veteran fire spotter. The spotting station is gone now, but at the time, whenever conditions warranted a human observer, Ken was sent to the mountaintop. Most summers he lived on the windswept peak from June to September.

Once slated as the ideal location for an astrological observatory, the clear air around Mount Kobau makes for some of the best star gazing in the world. The observatory was never built, but a good gravel road remains, the one that gives me easy access to a parking area just a one-kilometre hike from the lookout at the summit.

Ken's eyes are never still and one ear is always tuned to the intermittent chatter on his Forestry radio, yet he's happy to show visitors around. He patiently demonstrates the scope to a pair of young boys eager for a look. And inside the shack, he shows me the swivel firespotter, which has been in place since the station opened. The device sits on a map so that as Ken swings the sight to line it up with a target smoke plume he can read the bearing of the target off the azimuth ring in degrees.

He explains that establishing position is critical, especially when fire approaches a populated area. "That's the scariest part of my job," he says. "When it's in a residential area and houses are threatened I can order water bombers directly."

Lightning is the biggest villain. Ken shows me how he uses a marker on the window to record the position of strikes when a lightning storm comes through, so he can keep watch. "We call them layovers or sleepovers," he tells me, explaining that with lightning fires the accompanying rain knocks down the telltale smoke. "We may not see the fire for two or three days."

The 360-degree views from Mount Kobau are stupendous. Ken knows the massive expanse of terrain like the rest of us know our backyards. One by one he points out the sights. "That's Old Glory," he says, indicating a smudge on the distant horizon. "In the Kootenays." We can see Oliver and Osoyoos and directly below, a glistening white patch in the earth-tone landscape. Ken doesn't have to name the lake. I can see the spots.

Note: *The fire lookout on Mount Kobau was closed for many years and has now been completely removed, but the views are still stupendous.*

Ken Bushey
manning the
Mount Kobau
fire lookout in
August 2000.

Mother-in-law
Dinora Kemp proudly
h ked the summit
trail at age 91.

After finally spotting Spotted
Lake from the summit of
Mount Kobau, I stopped
by for a closer look.

Myra Canyon before 2003 fire. Facing Page: Trail Store between Naramata and Penticton.

Chapter 2

Kettle Valley Rail Trail

A LOT OF INK IN THIS BOOK is devoted to grumbling about
steep terrain and hiking trails that only seem to go up, so you can
appreciate my deep attachment to the Kettle Valley Rail Trail. Built for
rail transit in the age of steam, the former rail bed presents maximum
grades of around two per cent that seem all but imperceptible. With
segments readily accessible from Kelowna, Summerland, Penticton
and Naramata, the trail is ideal for local daytrips and overnighters.
And now that the KVR Trail forms part of one of the most beautiful
and popular sections of the Trans Canada Trail, the old rail line
has forged a modern link with regions beyond the valley.

Myra Canyon Trestles

RANDOM EVENTS PRODUCE SURPRISING RESULTS. In 1887, when prospectors found silver near Nelson, BC, territorial boundaries were far from a sure thing in this young country. With no direct rail line from the Kootenays through Canadian territory to the Coast, real fears arose that the region would follow the easy north-south trade route and become part of the United States.

Time for the ultimate Canadian solution—time for a railway.

Yet even feisty chief engineer Andrew McCulloch must have felt daunted by the magnitude of the project that eventually got started in 1910. Traversing nearly five hundred kilometres of some of the toughest terrain ever conquered during the age of steam, his creation, the Kettle Valley Railway, would justifiably come to be known as McCulloch's Wonder.

The rails are all gone now (except for a short section in Summerland used by the Kettle Valley Steam Railway), but the trail they left behind winds through country as rugged and picturesque as any traveller could hope to find. And I love the idea that McCulloch's achievement has made the transition to a new age of transportation, living on as the Kettle Valley Rail Trail (KVR Trail), now one of the most popular sections of the Trans Canada Trail.

Near Kelowna, the Myra Canyon section is iconic—as big a draw for locals as it is for visitors to the Okanagan or through riders and hikers. This section was one of McCulloch's biggest challenges. "Never saw a

At a Glance

Access to both ends of Myra Canyon starts on KLO Road. For Ruth Station take KLO to June Springs Road then Little White Forest Service Road. For Myra Station, stay on KLO past Gallagher's Canyon Golf Club to Myra Forest Service Road. Visitor centres stock pamphlets on the KVR and related tour operators. Recommended reading: *Kettle Valley Railway* by Gerry Doeksen; *Cycling the Kettle Valley Railway* by Dan & Sandra Langford; *Myra's Men: Building the Kettle Valley Railway—From Myra Canyon to Penticton* by Maurice Williams. Visit the Myra Canyon Restoration Society online at www.myratrestles.com/.

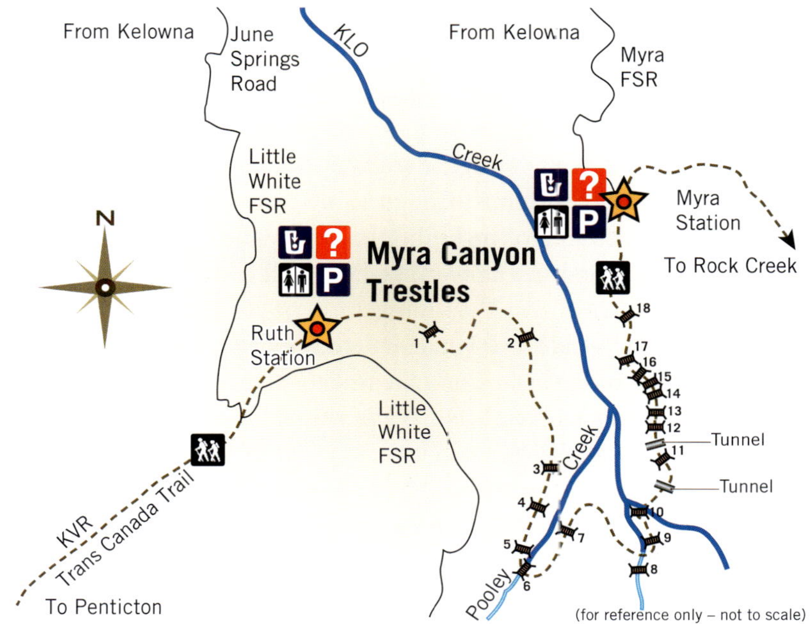

railway built on any such hillside as this! Cannot even guess the cost now," he wrote in his diary.

Although the canyon measures a mere 1.6 kilometres across its mouth, it took nearly nine kilometres of track, eighteen trestles and two tunnels to forge a train-friendly route around the rim. Day trippers head for the twelve-kilometre section between the former Myra and Ruth stations that bookend the canyon.

I've been "doing" the trestles since I moved to the valley in the early 1990s. My first encounter was a cycle trip with Dad (then seventy-something) whose inner mining engineer brimmed enthusiasm for McCulloch's design—and for explaining it to me (in *detail*). Each timber in the intricate latticework of canyon-taming trestles was hand cut and bored. No shims permitted, fitting had to be exact.

At the time, we were actually looking at the fourth generation of timber. The original Douglas fir structures had to be replaced about every fifteen years. It wasn't until the 1960s and 1970s that the wood was treated to last. And we owed a debt of gratitude to the Myra Canyon Restoration Society. With contributions of labour, funds and materials these local volunteers had installed decking and sturdy, comforting handrails. They also numbered the trestles starting at Ruth Station.

Originally this was known as Kelowna Station, but was soon rechristened (for McCulloch's younger daughter) to eliminate confusion with the city name. Bear with me through an overview of the trestle line-up in which I'll treat you to the highlights and subject you to a string of statistics only a died-in-the-wool railway buff (or an engineer) could love.

Between No. 1 and No. 2 you can detour off the railbed for a look at one of the rock ovens used along the line to bake bread for work crews during construction. Trestle No. 6 was the site of the last spike for the Carmi Subdivision, driven October 2, 1914. At 219.8 metres, this bridge is the canyon's longest and also the highest. Unless you have a head for heights, skip the 55.5-metre straight-down view into Pooley Creek. The current twelve-span steel bridge replaced the original wooden structure during upgrades undertaken when the CPR assumed operations in 1931.

At approximately the halfway point, trestle No. 7 forms an unusual s-curve with twelve-degree bends to the left and right. The second steel bridge, a five-span structure that was also part of the early 1930s upgrades, forms trestle No. 9.

Just beyond the next trestle a tunnel bores through eighty-four metres of solid canyon wall, then you're at the Carmi summit, 1,274 metres above the Pacific. After trestle No. 11 it's a downhill run to the second and longest tunnel (one hundred and fourteen metres of damp, drippy darkness).

From the curve at trestle No. 12, when you look across the canyon to the tightly spaced string of trestles No. 14 to No. 17, you're seeing a bit of movie history. During the 1973 filming of the CBC documentary *The National Dream*, Myra Canyon acted as the cinematic stand-in for the Fraser Canyon. Train sequences were shot here and at trestle No. 4.

Trestle No. 18 marks the beginning of the home stretch for Myra Station, which is also named for the daughter of a railway engineer, J.L. Newman.

Rock oven used by railway
workers to bake bread
during construction of the
KVR is located between
trestles No. 1 and No. 2.

Cne of two tunnels on the Myra
Canyon section of the KVR Trail.

Snowshoeing the Myra Canyon section of the KVR Trail in winter.

These memorials stood just off the trail in Myra Canyon. Destroyed during the 2003 Okanagan Mountain Park Fire, they have now been restored.

In January 2003, the Myra Canyon section of McCulloch's Wonder was designated a National Historic Site.

By then, the trestles and tunnels were thoroughly familiar to me. I'd made the pilgrimage every year, sometimes walking a section with visitors, sometimes cycling from Ruth to Myra and back (or the reverse). I'd shared a guided tour with co-workers and introduced the sights to my new man, Bruce, when he first moved west. A friend and I even tried snowshoeing the white path in winter. So the terrible days of early September 2003—the days of the Okanagan Mountain Park Fire—will always stick with me.

For nearly three weeks we'd lived with evacuation notices, choking smoke and roaring water bombers (I have a shot of a Mars Bomber about a hundred feet over my daughter's head as she walked through a downtown park in her wedding dress). News reports were finally taking on a positive note, even cautiously testing out the C-word, but just as we began to believe that fire fighters might truly have the monster contained, it made one last offensive and raced into Myra Canyon.

While the battle raged for days, it could only be a rearguard action as the focus shifted to turning the blaze before it leveled a nearby neighbourhood. When the smoke finally cleared (a terrible cliché, but perfectly accurate), the decks of the two steel structures were gone and twelve historic trestles were reduced to ash.

It's hard to convey the sense of loss I felt—that the whole community shared. This tragedy touched us personally.

So you'll appreciate our gratitude to the members of the Myra Canyon Restoration Society (again), who tackled the challenge of rebuilding our heritage. On June 22, 2008, the Myra Canyon section of the KVR Trail reopened.

As Bruce and I walked the familiar path a few days later, I was reminded of Dad's lecture on the original construction and felt sure that Andrew McCulloch would be proud of the latest iteration of his wonder.

KVR History/Archeology Tour

SINCE MY FIRST-YEAR UNIVERSITY classics course (Egyptian hieroglyphs, Greek pots ...) I've wanted to visit a dig site. Notice I didn't say I wanted to take part in a dig—all that meticulous sifting and dust-brushing—but I did really want to see the process of archeology in action. It never occurred to me that I'd get my chance here in the Okanagan.

Never mind that the UBC Okanagan students working under the direction of associate professor and archeologist Rick Garvin aren't going to stumble on another Tutankhamen's tomb, what they are turning up is some pretty cool stuff ... unearthing the detritus of the humble working men who laboured in the 1910s to build the Myra Canyon section of the Kettle Valley Railway.

The students are excavating a work camp and unearthing remnants of the everyday lives of the men—mainly poor immigrants—who lived there while they dug the tunnels and built the famous trestles that took the KVR around the rim of Myra Canyon.

The dig is part of a joint project involving Rick and his colleague, associate professor and historian, Maurice (Maury) Williams, who released the results of his research in 2008, a terrific book called *Myra's Men: Building the Kettle Valley Railway—From Myra Canyon to Penticton.*

I get my look at a dig because Kelowna Museums is partnering with the university to offer public tours that take in part of the KVR Trail (with Williams acting as interpreter and guide) along with a visit to the archeology site (hosted by Rick).

Getting there is a bit of a kidney-cruncher over a rough dirt track, likely first built as a tote road for the horse-drawn freight wagons that made the two-day trek up from Kelowna. Our trip feels only slightly

At a Glance

Guided tours of the Myra Canyon trestles and the UBC Okanagan Archeology and History Field School were so popular that first summer of 2008 that they've continued in successive years. Contact the Kelowna Museums for details.

shorter, being third in line and enveloped the entire way in a cloud of dust— (kind of like getting to a dig in Egypt?).

When we park and the cloud settles enough to reveal Rick (Indiana Jones in a straw hat), he explains that the camp was discovered by members of the Myra Canyon Trestle Restoration Society—one of those remarkable silver lining stories. Had they not been surveying the area after the 2003 Okanagan Mountain Park Fire destroyed twelve of the famous trestles, the camp might never have been found.

Passing around a historic photo that shows the camp in operation, Maury speculates that it likely functioned for about one year. Approximately one hundred men would have been in residence at any given time, rotating in and out from Kelowna. Turnover was high and there was a bonus for workers who stayed a full three months.

The men, mostly Poles, Galicians and Ukrainians, were supervised by American managers. They were working on the two Myra Canyon tunnels, which they dug by hand at the rate of around 1.5 metres per day, and erecting the prefab trestle sections that chief engineer Andrew McCulloch had built at Carmi and transported by rail to the site.

Rebuilt trestles look just like the ones destroyed in the 2003 forest fire. Note burned trees in the background.

Rick takes up the tag team narrative, explaining that the camp was established by George Chew (not Oriental—only a few Orientals working as cooks were involved in the KVR construction in this area). He was a contractor from Spokane, Washington, who operated twelve camps between Hydraulic (McCulloch) Lake and trestle No. 17.

After the intro the student diggers take us in hand, leading small groups around the site. Initially chainsaws and weed-whackers had to be used to clear the brush and reveal the symmetrical ridges that indicated building foundations. Work is under way on the bunkhouse with the area marked by string into two-metre squares and dotted by little flags pinpointing finds—orange for metal (cans, files, nails); yellow for glass (lamp chimneys, bottles) and pink for miscellaneous (ceramic, leather). Rick works the groups, stopping to show off a contraband liquor bottle.

Lindsay Canning, a fourth-year anthropology student and the leader of my group, shows us the full set of cutlery she uncovered. Most often she turns up nails, but her first find was a file. "I was using the trowel to dig and I heard a clunk. I said, 'Oh my god, I found something!'" She adds, "A file to most people is not much, but when you're looking at nails all day, a file is really something."

Lindsay's classmate, Les Miller, holds up another file and the rusty foot of a wood stove. It may not sound like much, but I sure feel the thrill.

UBC Okanagan anthropology student Lindsay Canning shows off the cutlery she uncovered in the archeological excavation of a KVR construction work camp.

Chute Lake to Penticton

THE MYRA CANYON TRESTLES GET A LOT OF PRESS. But there's another section of the KVR Trail that involves even more spectacular Okanagan scenery (my opinion), a genuine character, lunch at a Naramata Bench winery, a mind-bogglingly knowledgeable tour guide and one border collie.

"It's all downhill," Ed Kruger assures us as he packs people into, and mountain bikes on top of his Monashee Adventure Tours minibus. Comforting words for a couple of semi-out-of-shape middle agers like Bruce and me, joining a group of thirty-something Vancouver lawyers on a thirty-six-kilometre team building trek.

Ed's partner Buzz follows me to the back row of seats, drops down and plops his head on my lap. He prefers to ride shotgun, but when guests are on board he grudgingly makes way. Yes, Buzz is the collie.

He dozes happily, slobbering just a little, while his human pilots the minibus from Kelowna down the west side of Okanagan Lake, around the south end and into the high country above Naramata—dropping a stream of info nuggets along the way.

"Mt. Boucherie (a West Kelowna landmark) is an extinct volcano… Greata Ranch (now a winery) was once a stop for the S.S. Sicamous sternwheeler…Giant's Head Mountain (in Summerland) was dubbed Shaughnessy Head because it looked like the bearded face of Sir Thomas Shaughnessy, president of the CPR during construction of the Kettle Valley Railway—but the beard fell off in a landslide and the name went with it …"

At a Glance

Ed Kruger at Monashee Adventure Tours hosts the Rock Ovens to Valley Vistas trek and a variety of other itineraries summer and winter. This tour includes bike rental, helmet, snacks, lunch, transport, guide and canine companionship. Details at www.monasheeadventuretours.com. You can also arrange a do-it-yourself tour by taking a shutt e from Penticton to Chute Lake (use your own bike or rent) with a company like Ambrosia Tours www.ambrosiatours.ca.

You get the idea. If there's something Ed can't tell you about Okanagan history, it's probably not worth knowing.

We unload at Chute Lake Resort, a Red Green-style lodge, burger stop and tent ground favoured by hikers and cyclists doing the trail. (More on this later in the chapter.)

The group that piles out of the van looks a lot different from the first summer day trippers who might have ridden the rails on this route in 1915. Not an ankle-length muslin skirt or a twirling parasol in sight as Ed completes his circle checks—seat heights adjusted, helmets secure— and we push off.

Pedalling along the rail bed in the chilly morning air, it's fascinating to see the erratic legacy of the previous year's Okanagan Mountain Park Fire (2003). Both Bruce and I covered the aftermath of the monster burn at the Kelowna end. Whole neighbourhoods were reduced to smoldering ash save for a single home here and there that inexplicably escaped the devastation. It's the same in the forest.

Great swaths of black spikes and rock-strewn earth traverse the hills. But amid the throng of dead trees, their needles rusty as autumn leaves, surprising islands of green survive. It's heart stopping to see how close to the resort the final battle lines were drawn.

Wildfire is a natural event in the Okanagan. Everything that lives here is well adapted to the burning cycle (well, everything but humans). Lodgepole pine cones open with the heat, releasing seeds for regeneration, and thick bark protects ponderosa pine and older Douglas fir from all but severe crown fires like this one.

It's amazing to see nature's healing hand where clumps of spring-green fern already add a splash of colour to the monochrome moonscape. Still, we're glad to get past the fire zone and start riding through healthy forest.

The old rail bed remains in remarkably good shape. Wide tires and the comfortable seats on our Giant mountain bikes make easy work of the stony and sandy sections as we trundle through rock cuts where purple wildflowers have gained a toe-hold in the sheer walls. Descending the gentle 2.2 per cent grade, we clatter over cattle guards and thud across wooden bridges spanning fast-running creeks.

Ed signals a stop where a massive fallen-log bridge leads to a mound of rock and earth shaped like a beehive with a hole in the middle. From his bottomless stock of Okanagan info-bits he plucks yet another factoid.

"Italian workers, who constructed the mortarless stonework along the line, built these rock ovens to bake bread," he says. Sensible and tasty, nothing like their rocket-scientist co-workers who figured the quickest way to thaw nitro glycerin (needed to blast the ultra-hard rock in this area, but prone to freeze when left in the open during winter) was to pop it into a frying pan and give it a shake over the campfire. Fatalities were high.

Somehow these daredevils (or dumbbells) managed to complete the four hundred and eighty-nine metre Adra spiral tunnel that chief engineer Andrew McCulloch designed to tame the drop from Chute Lake to Penticton (eight hundred and fifty metres over twenty-four kilometres or a 4.5 per cent grade—not good for loaded trains).

Although we can't cycle through the Adra, we do have a peek in the entrance, blocked up in 1992 when the tunnel became unsafe. And skirting puddles formed by water dripping from the roof, we scoot through Little Tunnel, the line's shortest at just forty-nine metres.

McCulloch's switchbacks bring us from Douglas fir forest down through the ponderosa pine level of open parkland, with black-eyed Susans and blood-red poppies skirting the trail, out onto the mountain face with uninterrupted views up and down the valley. The sun warms our backs and we peel layers in the mounting heat.

On one leg the view is north past Summerland on the opposite shore. Then the trail makes a one-eighty and we're looking south across Naramata to Penticton on the narrow isthmus between Okanagan and Skaha lakes.

Buzz runs along beside the bikes, occasionally following his nose into the bush and rejoining us farther down the trail. He's absent when a grouse (eager for fame) steps onto the path. Bruce drops onto his belly for an eye-to-eye photo op. I (more sanely) wait until the bird hops onto a rock ledge and poses.

The ride takes about four hours, finishing off at Hillside Estate Winery where we're lucky to meet winemaker Kelly Symonds in the tasting room. Pouring a sample of Hidden Valley Rosé, she tells us, "We use the classic rosé method. It's a Merlot/Syrah blend left for seventy-two hours on the skins then bled off and made like a white."

This seems to mean something to the au courant among our cycle partners and Bruce nods sagely. I acknowledge a vague understanding, but mostly just accept that it tastes good—as does the crisp Pinot Gris and fruity Gewürztraminer. On the leafy patio of the rustic Barrel Room Bistro, we pair the suggested Muscat Ottonel with our Hillside wrap and soak up the scent of ripening cherries and earthy grapes with the warm sunshine and lake view. Mellow…the best of the Okanagan, and it was all downhill.

Note: This tour now runs between Chute Lake and Penticton with lunch at a waterfront restaurant.

Tour guide Ed Kruger on the KVR Trail looking north toward Peachland.

Photogenic grouse on the trail between Chute Lake and Naramata.

Chute Lake Resort

THE TITLE "RESORT" MIGHT GIVE a bit of a wrong impression here. Think *Red Green Show* and you'll be on the right track. The wood-burning stove, vinyl-covered seating and deer antler accessories would fit right in at Possum Lodge, although I wouldn't compare owners Gary and Doreen Reed with Red and his nasal nephew, Herold, except to say that their hospitality is legendary.

With the KVR/Trans Canada Trail running right by the door, hikers, cyclists and snowmobilers know this as a convenient stop for a burger or a night's rest. Anglers know Chute Lake for its natural spawn, pan-size trout and antiques fans know about Gary's eclectic trove. But Bruce and I sometimes make the trek just for a wedge of Doreen's delectable pie.

A run to the resort makes a good day trip up the mountain beyond Naramata. Okanagan Lake paints a blue backdrop for the leafy green of the east shore orchards and vineyards. And as the road climbs to Chute Lake at the 1,200 metre level, each switchback opens a new window. One minute you're looking south past Penticton, the next, Giant's Head Mountain stands tall over Summerland. Round another bend and the far ridges are receding into blue-grey haze beyond Peachland.

When you spot a tranquil mountain lake and a rambling log building fronted by a patch of lawn strewn with so many bikes and Lycra-clad bodies it looks like a waypoint on the Tour de France—you're there.

We pull in just around lunchtime on a Saturday in June. It's early enough in the season that we haven't made reservations for pie. Midsummer, when Doreen gets calls for thirty or more slices a day, that would be foolhardy. But we're okay. The golden circles are still warm from the oven and smell like cinnamon, fruit and grandma's kitchen.

Doreen stands behind the counter and presents a tantalizing dilemma— "apple or rhubarb." (Other times it's berries in season.) We exer-

At a Glance

To reach Chute Lake Resort by car, take the right fork where the road branches at Naramata. Signs point the way. For hikers/cyclists on the KVR/Trans Canada Trail, it's fifty kilometres from Myra Canyon and forty-two kilometres from Penticton.

cise exemplary problem solving skills and order cne of each—each. Ice cream topping is optional, but I call that a no-brainer.

To keep our salivary glands in check during the wait, we look around the room at some of Gary's famously wide-ranging collection. Flat irons sit on the windowsills, line crimpers hang on a wall plaque and sunlight shines through a row of glass insulators.

Insulators are what got him started. I guess the interest was natural enough, given his job as a career telephone lineman, and he isn't alone. Can you believe there's actually an International Insulator Club? Of course Gary joined up, but even as he pursued this passion, his eye began to wander.

"I jumped over to fruit and canning jars," he says, "then old gas engines and farm machinery, and '40s and '50s long-neck beer bottles. Emptied some of those myself (sheepish grin)."

Gary admits that long necks aren't such a big deal any more since breweries have returned to that style, but he's got lots of other goodies in the sheds behind the lodge. When our plates are all but licked clean, we wander out to see what might be new among the rows of prized insulators, legions of BC license plates, antique gas station signs, vintage sewing machines and wooden yokes.

"I started collecting around 1970," says the compulsive accumulator whose inventory keeps growing. "Collectors buy from me, but, it's still just a hobby, so I don't care about turnover." (Good thing.)

He cranks up a one-lung motor that roars a steady thumpa-thumpa as he points out the 2.5 horsepower Johnson Seahorse hanging from the rafters. One of his prize possessions is a cast-iron woodstove that once heated the KVR station in Summerland. Another is a 1952 Chrysler Imperial with power windows and seats that still work. Everything is for sale, and maybe someday a KVR trekker will chuck his bike in the cavernous trunk and drive that beauty home.

For me, though, it's still all about the pie.

Note: *I've recently heard that the resort could be up for sale. By the time you read this, Doreen's pie may be just a blissful memory.*

Octogenarian mountain goat clearing trail. Facing Page: Okanagan Lake looking south from Peachland Trails.

Chapter 3

Winter Tracks

WHEN I WAS A KID on my grandparents' farm in Ontario, one of my chief joys was rummaging in the barn for the treasures my packrat family stored away. Many of the artifacts came from the north where my great-grandfather was chief forest ranger in Temagami from 1910 to 1935 and in the later years my grandfather his deputy chief. Summers, the families lived on Bear Island, well up Temagami Lake, close to the forest fire action. But in winter, they returned to the ranger station on a small island just off the town. As soon as the ice was solid enough, my mother could walk to school using a pair of child-sized snowshoes made for her by the local Ojibwa people. Those snowshoes were the most exciting treasures I found in that barn. I'd strap the leather thongs around my brown rubber slip-over-your-shoes winter boots and trek among the bare-branched apple trees and across the open fields, playing all the characters in the stories I concocted as I walked. Many decades later and half a country away, I've reconnected with my love of snowshoeing.

Peachland Trails and Jim's Trail

MY DAD THE MOUNTAIN GOAT is a terrestrial version of James T. Kirk, "boldly going where no man has gone before." Early in our hiking partnership I learned that Dad prefers the trail less travelled, or more accurately, the trail (and I'm using the term very loosely here) not travelled at all.

Over the years this penchant for bushwhacking has led us through minefields of hip-high windfalls tangled like a giant game of pick-up-sticks; across the face of all but perpendicular talus slopes, each boot plant an adventure in lost footing; up and over an endless range of coronary inducing Everests. The fact that I managed to survive this nightmare of accidents in waiting, only to feel the fatal snap of my left fibula on an open trail in a regional park, remains for me a source of deep embarrassment.

But the old goat has to fess up to a red face now and then too. Without recounting all the details, let's just say that more than once our perilous passage brought us out at or near a perfectly safe and, dare I say, well-travelled trail.

Dad first introduced me to the Peachland Trails years ago. Lookout Ridge delivers one of the best views in the valley—a sweeping panorama of the big bend in Okanagan Lake from Kelowna to Summerland. The broad clearing on the point is a super picnic spot with a fire pit and shady bench. Year round access makes the five-kilometre loop an ideal half-day for hikers, snowshoers, cyclists and horseback riders.

At a Glance

To reach Peachland Trails, turn west at the Princeton Avenue/Hwy 97 traffic light in Peachland. Drive 8.7 kilometres to the trailhead—the last couple on gravel where Princeton Avenue turns into Brenda Mine Road. The parking area is a large clearing on the right (north) side. Look for the trail marker and aerial map posted on a tree a little way into the bush. The main trail is well marked with green hiker signs. The lookout clearing is along a short side trail. Before using the fire pit, make sure burning is currently permitted and before you leave, be sure your fire is out!

You won't find Jim's Trail marked on a map, and I'm going to keep this personal treasure to myself. Sorry.

(for reference only – not to scale)

For my money, though, the best season for this trail is winter, especially when falling snow deadens all sound and long-ago logged tree stumps wear steadily growing white toques. After a fresh snowfall it's easiest to see the tales of life in the forest—dainty deer trails, deep moose prints, rabbit and coyote tracks, sometimes ending in a tellingly dramatic jumble, and early enough in the winter, the human hand sized impressions of padded bear paws.

Some mornings, when hoar frost coats bare branches, evergreen needles and hanging moss, the forest morphs into a crystal palace. Most times, valley cloud and floating mist create a moody scene from the lookout and it's a rare treat on sunny winter days when blue sky echoes from the lake.

One winter I followed the mountain goat on a quest to find a side trail that shows on the topo map, but isn't posted onsite. GPS and orienteering skills notwithstanding, we couldn't find it and the outing turned into yet another adventure in bushwhacking. That spring he returned by himself and with the snow gone, managed to find the track, even though it was heavily overgrown. A week later he was back with his trusty axe and by the next snowfall, had a new trail to show me.

I find this compulsion to hack an easily walkable path through the forest somewhat at odds with the Dad's inner bushwhacker, but there it is. His most recent foray into trail blazing occupied much of the summer and fall of 2009 and involved his inner engineer. A summer trail in the hills not far from the city where we live leads to a series of terrific viewpoints overlooking Okanagan Lake. Even in hiking boots, parts of this trail are a rough climb, but in snowshoes, it's pretty much out of the question.

So Dad takes it into his head to map out a route with manageable grades and proceeds to clear deadfalls, hack back the undergrowth and on steep side hills (with some help from his buddy Herb) shore up a new path. My first snowshoe trek around the new loop I've dubbed Jim's Trail, leaves me gasping at the size of the deadfalls he'd tackled single-handed with the chainsaw he had to carry in.

We're about half way around when he suggests a little detour (uh-huh). The snow is deep and I'm puffing like a steam engine even though he's the one breaking trail, when he suddenly steps aside. We're standing at the edge of a tiny clearing, not ten metres from a perfect little log cabin.

I should point out that, to me, every log cabin is perfect, regardless how close to total collapse. One of my greatest pleasures in exploring the Okanagan backcountry is stumbling on these remarkably abundant historic remnants. European settlement was so recent here that log cabins built by homesteaders, ranchers and men working on irrigation works are often still in remarkably good condition.

Sadly, this feature that made Jim's Trail even more special, is gone, burned to ash by the regional district in the spring of 2010.

The log cabin on Jim's Trail was burned down in 2010 soon after this photo was taken.

Snow ghost gets a good laugh at my expense.

Peachland Trails lookout. The view includes Okanagan Mountain on the other side of Okanagan Lake.

Kelowna Nordic and Telemark Cross-Country Ski Clubs

SINCE MY THIRTIES, when I learned to downhill on the angled skating rinks that pass for ski hills in Ontario, I've appreciated the positive role that gravity can play in winter sports. It's not that I'm lazy (well, maybe it is), but the very idea of skiing *up*hill leaves me scratching my head. Especially here in the Okanagan where we have such great gravity-assisted terrain, with actual snow—I'm talking fluffy powder. Hop on a lift, strike up a friendly conversation with whoever's sharing the chair and—whoosh—I'm at the top of the world ready to glide down the nice tame greens and blues. Civilized.

So what's the deal with these Nordic types, the Lycra-skinned human muscles who (to my everlasting amazement) herringbone up virtual cliff faces for the sole purpose of freeheeling down what I call black diamond madness. Seriously—how do they do that? More to the point—why do they do it?

I raised these questions with the mountain goat parental unit who started cross-country skiing in his late seventies. Nowhere in his response did I find motivation to reveal the extent of my personal jour-

At a Glance

The Kelowna Nordic Cross-Country Ski Club maintains about seventy kilometres of trails for all levels and disciplines of cross-country skiers (with a maximum vertical of 235 metres), a K-9 route for Rover, chalet and warming cabins and over forty kilometres of snowshoe trails. The club is located adjacent to the KVR Trail/Trans Canada Trail near McCulloch (Hydraulic) Lake, thirty-eight kilometres southeast of Kelowna off Hwy 33. Visit www.kelownanordic.com for rates and trail maps. In summer, the area is known as the Mildred Wardlaw Nature Trails.

Telemark Cross-Country Ski Club grooms over fifty kilometres of trails for classic and skate skiing and offers night skiing, biathlon range, chalet, rentals, lessons and forty kilometres of snowshoe trails. The climb from the chalet to Crystal Rim Trail is 225 metres. Exit Hwy 97 at the Glenrosa interchange in West Kelowna and follow Glenrosa Road north for nine kilometres. Visit www.telemarkx-c.com for rates and trail maps.

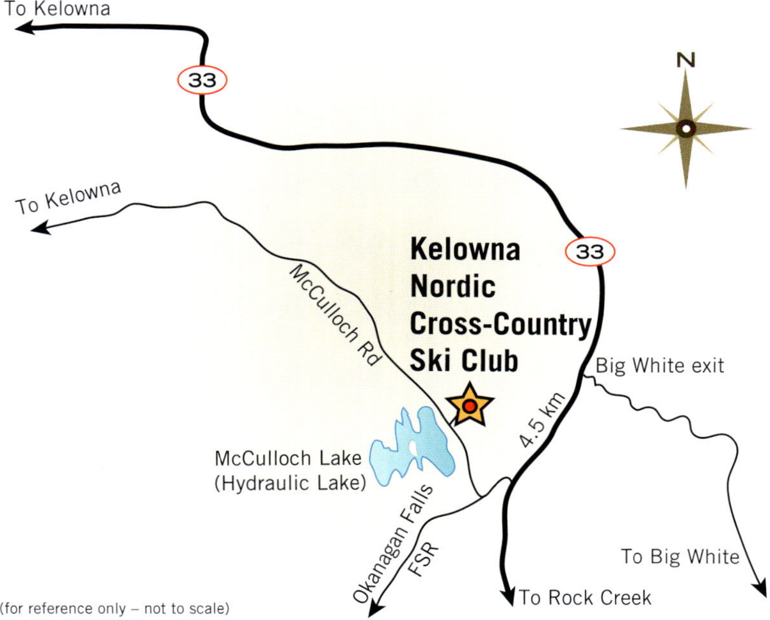

ney into middle-age spread by donning one of those Star Trek suits. And I definitely saw no sane reason for working my butt off to subject my increasingly brittle bones to certain disaster.

You need to know that I'm the highly coordinated individual who managed to break her leg on a hiking trail—and did I mention my last downhill run at Big White. You can't image how much less appealing that fluffy powder can be when it's flipping into your face from the tails of the safety patroller's snow-plowing skis—causing blurred vision and near asphyxiation from clogged nostrils as you lie trussed like a Christmas turkey in the rescue basket with a bum knee. Why up the ante? Bring on the nice stable snowshoes, I say.

And so it transpires that on my man Bruce's first Christmas morning in the valley, he discovers a very large oblong package under the tree. Game to prove his devotion by waddling (nothing personal, everybody waddles on snowshoes) through the snowy woods and with the promise of a feast on the real trussed up turkey, he accompanies me without a whimper, enthusiastically even, to the Kelowna Nordic Cross-Country Ski Club east of Kelowna near McCulloch (known officially as Hydraulic) Lake. By a strange quirk of fate—well, geography, really—it happens that many of the Okanagan's most popular snowshoe trails are located at Nordic ski clubs.

Christmas Day 2006, we have a choice of six trails totalling forty-two kilometres plus as much of the adjacent KVR Trail as we choose to trek. Since then the club has cleared twelve more trails for up to seventy-two kilometres of snowshoeing bliss.

But these days we can stick closer to home with Telemark Cross-Country Ski Club twenty minutes from our back door. In the last few years they've cleared about forty kilometres of snowshoe trails—including some ridiculous verticals that I leave to the geriatric mountain goats.

Bruce snowshoeing the KVR Trail near Kelowna Nordic.

Snowshoe Safari

WINTER STRUCK AROUND FIFTEEN HUNDRED METRES. It's a phenomenon that always amazes this native flatlander—elastic seasons dependant more on altitude than calendar. When I pulled out of my driveway this morning yellow and purple blossoms lined the border. But about half way up the road to Vernon's Silver Star Mountain Resort I cross the snowline—and how.

Jumbo flakes drop like parachutists on a mission, obliterating the blacktop in rapidly deepening layers. In places the nose of my little Toyota is plowing. Pretty good omen for a snowshoe safari. And I'm looking forward to this ladies' day on the mountain guided by my favourite walking Wikipedia. I've trekked with Roseanne Van Ee in search of wildflowers and wild mushrooms, so I'm curious to see what wildness she'll root out of a snowdrift.

Roseanne told me to meet the group in Silver Star village at Valhalla Pure Outfitters where I find a couple of other early arrivals already browsing through the racks of snow duds. Temptation overcomes me and before she turns up, I've laid down plastic for a snappy woolen head warmer. What could I do? Most hats make me look like a refugee from the merchant marine (could be my penchant for watch caps), but this little number … too much information?

When we're fully assembled (and the last purchase bagged), our leader quickly kits the seven other women with lightweight, quick release snowshoes (I have my own). She marches us into the nostril-sticking, breath-misting morning and, mercifully, beyond the amused glances of graceful sliders and gliders, before helping us mount up.

At a Glance

Silver Star snowshoe tours often involve a culinary element—cider, chocolate, buffet lunch or gourmet dinner. Seems like a reasonable reward for strapping those contraptions to your feet and trekking through the silent, snowbound forest—or maybe that's reward enough. Check out www.outdoordiscoveries.com for details on tours: mid-day, sunset, dinner, New Year's, Valentine's, St. Patrick's and ladies' days. Register at Valhalla Pure Outfitters on Silver Star at 250.558.4292.

Arty twig on a winter trail.

We stand in a ragged line, some looking at the metal and vinyl plat-ters strapped to their feet with open anxiety. "Don't worry about walk-ing in them," Roseanne says. "It's like you woke up too early, all groggy, and put on somebody else's big slippers … but don't care."

"Easy for you," some of the faces say, but everybody's still game and our little group, mostly locals from Vernon, Enderby and Armstrong bolstered by a lone New Zealander and me, follow her lead. For the first two hundred metres we look like a string of giant toddlers in need of a diaper change, but the awkwardness fades and the newbies are soon striding confidently.

Conditions are stellar—about a foot of new powder in the bush without a track on it. We skip the groomed trails and head cross-coun-try. Fresh snow coats the trees and transforms the streamers of hanging lichen into garlands of angel hair. The going is tough, even with Rose-anne breaking trail, unless you're pulling up the rear—which I most-ly do (need to be at the back to photograph the group, you know). We have to lift our feet six or eight inches with each step—carrying the added weight of the snowshoes and also the load of snow that invariably piles on the decks when it's fresh and powdery like this.

But Roseanne knows about pacing and around the time I'm getting to thinking my desk-jockey lungs will burst, she calls a halt and gathers us around for a mini-lecture. One time she stops beside a larch tree and shows us how the Okanagan and Shuswap people would bend the long, slender branches to make their snowshoe frames, stringing the decks with catgut—cougar, lynx or bobcat (furtive over-the-shoulder glances).

On a steep open slope the trivia queen calls another halt plus a left turn. We now stand shoulder-to-shoulder looking across the valley at Camelback Mountain. A lesson in volcanology follows, including a quick history of the forty-million year old cone.

"Now stand quiet and listen," Roseanne orders. "Hear that?"

Ears strain into the thick silence.

"We can hear Laurie's heartbeat."

And we can! Now that's quiet (or near-fatal).

Lots of places we have to get down inclines that look to me like double black diamond ski runs. The technique Roseanne explains—ava-

Sleigh ride from Wild Horseman's Cabin to Silver Star village.

lanche running—is every bit as hair-raising as it sounds. Head straight downhill, keep your snowshoe tips up and take short steps—or turn into a human snowball.

She cautions that this only works in deep powder where each step causes a mini-avalanche, forming a deep enough pile of snow to give you a foothold—as long as you keep moving. Right, you first.

Picture eight kids screaming and laughing on the toboggan hill—add a few years (okay, decades) and you've got the picture. Where the snow isn't deep enough for Roseanne's kamikaze run, we take the most intuitive route—bum down, shoes up. More screaming.

Eventually we emerge from the forest onto a groomed trail a couple of hundred metres from the rustic Wild Horseman's Cabin. Blinded the moment I walk through the door (foggy glasses), I don't need to see anything to feel welcome—toasty warmth, a tang of wood smoke, yummy smells.

Chef Adam is ready with baguettes warming in the oven, gourmet tomato soup bubbling on the cast-iron stove and a buffet laid with salad and veggies, dill roast potatoes and cheesy (that's a good thing) lasagna. Roseanne raids her backpack and produces a bottle of wine. Conversation abruptly stops. Much munching...

But I have to jump up from the feast and grab my camera when Adam points out the window at our return transport trotting down the trail—Fred and Barney—a pair of muscle-bound Belgians, drawing a bright red sleigh with a weathered cowboy (mega-Stetson) at the reigns. Talk about a Norman Rockwell moment.

Gerry the cowboy pulls a chair up to the table and joins in the now voluble chatter (ever notice how conversation levels rise in inverse proportion to the amount of food on plates), which climaxes when a bald eagle sails by, not ten metres from the window.

Although the sleigh ride back to the village is optional, Fred and Barney have a full load. I'm guessing nobody wants to face those black diamond pitches in reverse. And who could pass up the chance for a velvet smooth ride through a crisp afternoon, wafts of vapour rising from two powerful backs, the air scented with fir and pine (and the occasional meadow muffin) and a sit-down comic routine from our peerless driver. Snowshoeing is *so* tough.

Lunch is waiting at Wild
Horseman's Cabin.

Tour guide
Roseanne Van Ee helps
newbies buckle into
their snowshoes.

Roseanne calls this
avalanche running.
I call it crazy (fun).

Snowshoe Ice Fishing

I LOVE ICE FISHING. Actually, let me clarify just slightly. I love to *go* ice fishing. The fact is, I've never so much as dipped a line—and forget about threading a worm on a hook. For me, ice fishing is really just an excuse to strap on a pair of snowshoes and join the parental unit and the hubby, tromping across a forest-fringed white plain to spend the morning standing beside a black hole (watching them wash bait) with the winter sun warming my apple cheeks and a thermos of rum-laced coffee warming my innards. It's downright spiritual—except maybe, for the drippy nose.

Easy leap, then, to see why I'm so eager to sign up for Monashee Adventure Tours snowshoe ice fishing. Not only does this outing promise a high country high (thanks, John Denver), but since I've done a couple of KVR bike rides with Monashee's main man, Ed Kruger, I know it's going to be a good time.

The snowshoes are already loaded when I join the group piling into his van. Ed's second-in-command, the most personable border collie you're likely to meet, is a little miffed that one of the paying customers has snagged the passenger seat. But Buzz is pretty gracious about riding shotgun from the floor—tongue lolling, eyes alert, ears perked to catch the conversation.

Running north on the highway to Lake Country, Ed lets loose with his signature stream of factoids. Dilworth Mountain is named for a rancher; the town of Kelowna was originally bounded by Harvey Avenue, Richter Street, Clement Avenue and Okanagan Lake; Duck Lake takes its name from its shape . . .

We've turned east and climbed through bald cattle range into ponderosa parkland when Ed stops the van and points into the airy forest. "One of the trees in there was a seedling in 1695," he says. It's on pri-

At a Glance

Visit Buzz online and learn all about Ed Kruger's other winter tours at www.monasheeadventuretours.com. Along with the snowshoe options, he's now doing a thing with snowbikes (not a misprint) at Big White Resort and Knox Mountain in Kelowna.

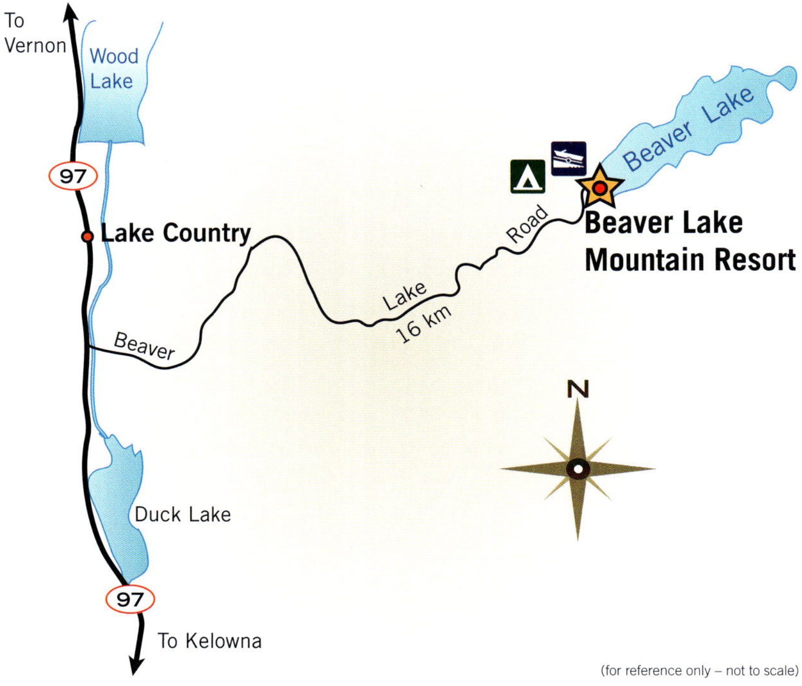

(for reference only – not to scale)

vate land, so we can't jump out and see for ourselves, but Ed assures us the old giant stands forty-one metres tall and measures nearly five metres around at the base. "It takes three guys stretched fingertip to fingertip to give it a bear hug."

Moving on toward Beaver Lake we round a series of switchbacks, each suddenly revealing an alternate view: Okanagan Lake—Oyama—Okanagan Lake … Up we climb into the Douglas fir zone where the trees are thick as the hair on a dog's back and snow pods on the branches give them the look of Christmas trees decorated in meringues.

Our destination, Beaver Lake Mountain Resort, has drawn fishing fanatics for generations. Bing Crosby and Bob Hope were regulars in the 1920s (another Ed-bit). As we pull in, Adrian Hasler, who was the fishing guide at the time and now owns and operates the property with his wife Daniela and son Jeremy, turns out to greet us.

A transplant from Switzerland, Adrian baited his first hook as a pre-schooler. "We'll be fishing close to shore where there're weeds under the ice," he explains, leading our little troop off terra firma. At least one or two members of the group clearly don't give a fig for weeds, they're just glad we aren't venturing too far out.

It's windy up on the plateau, leaving only a token cover of snow on the ice. We don't need our snowshoes and just crunch after Adrian to a spot about twenty metres from shore. He shows us the basic tools of the ice fisher. A hand auger (no wimpy power tools for this guy); a short rod with a simple hook and jaunty red and white bobber; a plastic container that looks to be filled with sawdust but also conceals a selection of irresistible (right) fish bait; and an egg flipper—no explanation.

Linda takes the bait (couldn't resist) when Adrian asks for volunteers to have a go with the auger. Makes for a good photo op, but fortunately we don't have to wait for her to grind through the ice. Fully prepared, Adrian kneels beside one of his pre-drilled holes and clears the skin of black ice—with the egg flipper.

Despite his best sales job, he can't hook anybody for bait duty (okay, I'll stop now), so he threads the big mealworms and passes out the rods. Buzz keeps a close watch on the proceedings. I'm not sure if he hopes to get in on a catch or just likes the little red and white bobby thing.

The others take turns jigging the lines (I have to keep my record clean), which makes Buzz very happy but has no perceptible impact on the fish. I harbour a mental image of a whole family of trout schooled just below the ice, looking up through the hole at the circle of faces peering hopefully into the black water. If fish can laugh, I'm sure they're killing themselves. Just no suicides by hook.

Doesn't matter. We all get to share in that standing-around-on-a-forest-fringed-white-plain experience I mentioned. No rum in the coffee (you let us down there, Ed) but a thoroughly fun time. And this is just the start.

For a real belly laugh, you have to watch a bunch of rookies strapping into snowshoes. But under Buzz's supervision, Ed soon has everybody kitted up and we waddle off. It's not really necessary to walk like this, you just tend to overreact until you get used to the extra-wide foot thing.

Ed breaks trail and we follow in line astern as he leads us through a deeply shadowed corridor of firs with a narrow blue ceiling, along the rim of snow-trimmed Vernon Creek and around the shoreline of the lake. Although the air feels sharp as it hits my lungs, I soon have to unzip my jacket and peel off the gloves.

We don't talk as we walk. All I hear is the swish-swish of weatherproof pant legs, the shush-shush of mushing snowshoes and the occasional chick-chick of an unseen whisky-jack scolding us for breaking the silence.

Along the way Ed stops to interpret dramatic stories in the snow. Evenly spaced holes with little triangular drag-marks (long-legged moose punching through the drifts); wide, troughs (muskrats or beavers); otter prints scooting in and out of the creek; snowshoe hare clusters; and mice tracks that suddenly stop in a flurry of wing marks. Ouch!

The critter condo—an evergreen sapling about a metre tall and all but buried in the snow—proves cheerier. Ed pulls aside a weighted branch to reveal the snug, snow-free space at the base of the young tree where weasels and otters and even little birds can shelter in climate-controlled comfort some degrees above freezing.

At our turn-around point Buzz supervises as Ed brakes out the hot chocolate (alas, still no rum) and we debrief.

"I was really amazed at how light the snowshoes are."

"I thought it'd be more awkward, but it was just like walking—after the first forty-five seconds."

"At first I was looking down a lot, then I realized I could look ahead—it's so beautiful."

"Didn't take long to gain confidence."

"It was fun to be able to go off trail, in around the trees. It felt like you were eavesdropping on the little creatures."

"I felt this is what it was like for people a hundred years ago ... I wonder if I'd have been a good pioneer."

Buzz doesn't much care about the philosophical speculation. He's bounding around with a stick in his mouth begging for a thrower.

Eventually a roil of pewter clouds threatens to blot out the sun and we aim our webbed feet back toward the van. Hint for travelling home with Buzz: don't sit in the second row. He likes to ride there with his paws on your lap. Very cosy—until the snow melts.

On the trail near
Beaver Lake.

Adrian Hasler from Beaver Lake
Mountain Resort baits the
hook for ice fishing rookies.

Waterfall and wildflowers in Cathedral Provincial Park. Facing Page: Swallowtail butterfly

Chapter 4

Mountain Flower Power

BRUCE INTRODUCED ME TO GARDENING, possibly regretting this very much whenever he wants to hold hands and all I can offer is a sandpaper-skinned paw with earth-blackened nails. I spend a lot of time with my fingers in the dirt. In spring, he gamely drives with me to the garden centre and the man is oh-so-gentle in pointing out that I've selected enough bedding plants to transform Drought Mountain. I grudgingly return a few to the shelves and buy yet more pots to handle the overflow. I need to explain that our garden space would probably fit in your living room, so there are limitations, which I annually fail to comprehend. Happily, my flower fetish finds an alternative outlet every time I lace up my hiking boots. And even if I weren't into trekking mountain meadows, I'd only need to look to the roadside as I drive around the Okanagan. Bring on the flowers.

Cathedral in the Sky

A MIDDLE-AGED WOMAN in multi-pocketed safari shorts, festooned in backpack and cameras, emerges from the treeline onto a flower carpeted alpine meadow. She flings wide her arms, twirls rapturously and bursts into a spontaneous chorus of *The Sound of Music.*

Okay, no actual singing (or twirling, for that matter)—but I'm here to tell you that Cathedral Provincial Park is a place of such spiritual beauty that the temptation is nearly overwhelming. St. Peter's may be bigger and St. Paul's more historic, but you won't convince me that this thirty-three thousand hectare wilderness enclave between the North Cascades and Okanagan Mountains isn't one of the most spectacular cathedrals in the world.

Before my first encounter, I learned from brochures and the web about the network of trails connecting six emerald and turquoise lakes: Quiniscoe, Ladyslipper, Scout, Pyramid, Glacier and Lake of the Woods. I knew of the soaring granite ramparts and monumental geological formations, yet words and pictures hopelessly failed to prepare me for the moment of emerging from the highest reaches of the Engleman spruce and Douglas fir forest onto a vast floral meadow more than two kilometres above the Pacific. Utterly breathtaking (and nothing to do with the mountain goat climb or oxygen deprivation at over 2,500 metres).

My alpine epiphany is due in large part to the vision of a single man. In 1934, Herb Clark purchased two parcels of land in what is now the

At a Glance

Cathedral Provincial Park and Protected Area provides a wilderness experience with limited access. Three trails lead to the core area, but it's a daylong climb that should only be attempted by fit and well-prepared hikers. Visit www.env.gov.bc.ca/bcparks for info including trail map. Cathedral Lakes Lodge, located on the shores of Quiniscoe Lake near the campsites in the core area, offers rooms in a Bavarian-style lodge as well as cabins and a bungalow. Meals and four-by-four transportation are included. Campers and day trippers can arrange transportation for a fee. For details see www.cathedral-lakes-lodge.com.

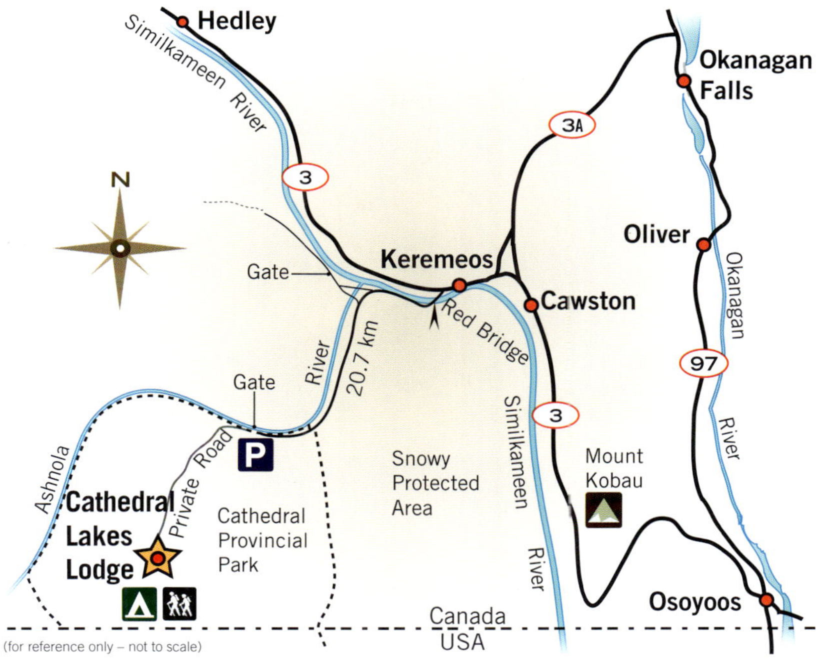

core area of the park. He built a pair of log cabins on Quiniscoe Lake and began offering a horseback guiding service. His operation gradually expanded, he took on partners and by the 1960s a private road provided limited vehicular access.

Since visitors tended to experience reactions much like my own, a grassroots movement emerged, dedicated to preserving the region in its natural state. The BC Government responded in 1968 by designating Cathedral Lakes a wilderness area provincial park.

Now over seven thousand visitor nights are recorded each summer—a factoid I glean from a park ranger one late-June afternoon as she grabs a short rest and a few rays on the front steps of the log cabin ranger station. Much of the time she's working hard to repair the damage all this human activity inflicts on an ecosystem that measures its growing season in weeks.

Over several years, park staff collected and planted native seeds in a revegetation program that's making steady gains. I see the new growth in roped off spaces throughout the core area. And a lot of work has also

Ladyslipper Lake in late June.

This mountain goat walked to within a couple of metres of us in Stone City on the Rim Trail.

been done on all-weather trails with the installation of boardwalks and bridges to keep hikers from detouring around boggy areas or damaging the creeks. Dogs and bikes aren't allowed in the park and tent pads reduce the human impact on campsites.

I'm proud to say that I also do my bit to keep camping areas in top condition by booking into Cathedral Lakes Lodge. This rustic assemblage of main building, bungalow and cabins on the shores of Quiniscoe Lake is no five-star resort, but even with shared bath facilities, it beats canvas walls and pit toilets by a wide margin. There's even a wood-fired hot tub—very beneficial for trail-weary muscles (trust me on this, I know what I'm talking about).

The big common room with its stone fireplace and overstuffed sofas would be a cliché if it didn't feel so welcoming. Hikers who invariably float back to camp on an endorphin high (or is that altitude sickness) invariably congregate here to relive the highlights of their day. Sometimes a little one-upmanship creeps into these conversations with claims of record-setting hike times and comparisons of mountain goat pics, at which point a certain element of lens envy usually kicks in. Meal times are also casual with open seating at big round tables and buffet style service that carries on the social atmosphere that started with the ride up the mountain.

Purists, who insist on packing their own gear on the six- to eight-hour, 1,100-metre climb to the park core, miss out on this adventure. Everyone else congregates at base camp beside the Ashnola River where you stash your wheels in a locked compound and switch to group transport. Even when I travelled solo, by the end of the four-by-four drive up what's euphemistically described as the access "road," I'd be feeling quite close to my new hiking buddies. It's impossible not to get chummy when you jostle shoulders and thighs for an hour.

On one trip, I met a young couple from Germany and a family from Ontario. Next time, it was a pair of retirees from Vancouver and a lady railway engineer. Most recently I've been making the trip with my husband Bruce and a group from Okanagan College on the annual Cathedral Lakes photography retreat that he hosts.

It's well worth the kidney-crunching ride to the park core where over sixty kilometres of marked trails radiate from the campgrounds and lodge at Quiniscoe Lake in the shadow of Pyramid Mountain. Unlike its counterparts in the Cascades and Rockies, Cathedral's highlights can easily be reached on one-day hikes. Ideally, you want a minimum of three days to explore, but if you're only up for a day trip—*and* you're pretty fit—head for the Rim Trail.

On my debut run-at-the-rim I hike with the lady railway engineer—a match made in heaven. Another compulsive photographer, she doesn't freak when I want to stop every fifty metres for another shot (and I'm equally gracious).

We capture all the icons: Glacier and Ladyslipper lakes, nestled in their separate valleys; the Devil's Woodpile, a sheer-faced cliff of columnar basalt; and Stone City, with its rounded, house-sized boulders, balanced precisely on top of each another like prehistoric condos. We stop here for lunch, feeling like an athletic Betty Rubble and Wilma Flintstone out for a picnic. At the Giant Cleft I scramble into position for what looks like a death defying pose while my partner gamely perches on the edge of infinity for my shot of Smokey the Bear.

From the rim itself we look east beyond the Okanagan Valley to the Kootenays then turn to the west and behold Mount Baker in the Cascades. A topographer, who once made the trip with Herb Clark, estimated the diameter of the circle in view at over eight hundred kilometres.

Completing the rim circuit is tough going in places with some prolonged, steep downhill sections that leave my not-in-shape-enough legs feeling like spaghetti and my big toenails so bruised, they're black and blue for six months.

Different hikes lead to hidden waterfalls, woodland streams and cold water lakes full of hungry trout. Until this summer (2010) I was totally miffed when practically all the other hikers came in with tales of spectacular sightings of mountain goats, adding insult to injury by cruelly showing off their awesome photos—but now I have bragging rights of my own. I still haven't spotted any of the shy little picas that squeak and scold from among the rocks (happily everybody else comes up short with these guys as well). But I'd have to be walking blindfolded to miss the marmots, birds and butterflies.

The last couple of years, however, my visits to Cathedral have been tinged with regret. It's heartbreaking to see a terrible change in the landscape that (for once) isn't manmade. Spruce beetles have invaded the forest, killing massive stands of trees, transforming lakeside vistas and presenting the rangers with a whole new set of challenges. Not that I see this as any reason to stay away. When I do that *Sound of Music* thing above the treeline, the views are still stupendous. And as far as I'm concerned, the profusion of tiny blossoms that bravely face biting winds and harsh environment to transform the alpine meadows each fleeting summer still make this our cathedral in the sky.

Dramatic perch overlook-
ing Glacier Lake from the
Rim Trail. Eight hours,
twelve kilometres and
four hundred metres
elevation gain. Mercy!

Canoes at Cathedral
Lakes Lodge on Quinis-
coe Lake in Cathedral
Provincial Park.

Silver Star Summer

"THE INDIAN PAINTBRUSH IS REALLY SPECTACULAR," says Roseanne Van Ee, the veteran guide who runs many of her Outdoor Discoveries nature tours at Silver Star Mountain Resort in Vernon. She credits generous spring sunshine for the early start to the blossom season. And this is a woman who really knows her wildflowers—and trees—and rocks …

Three hours on a mountain trail with Roseanne is better than a guided hike through your nature library. And you don't have to be an Edmund Hillary-clone to enjoy it. This tour is designed for the climbing-averse with an easy-rider ascent.

I execute a proficient butt-first entry as the chairlift scoops me up for the trip to the top. I've seen plenty of mountain terrain from this vantage point, but usually bundled to the eyeballs, skis dangling, battling snow blindness from the glare off the slopes. This experience is completely different, facing a landscape painted in multi-hues of green with broad brush strokes of exuberant wildflowers, desperate to attract attention in the short subalpine summer. And I'm hoping to spot a black bear—something in a close encounter of the aerial kind—with no potential for fang-in-flesh contact.

Alas, no bear. But there's no time for disappointment with Roseanne leading the troop. From the moment I step off the lift, I'm bowled over by her non-stop enthusiasm. "I really enjoy the natural environment and showing people about it," she says. "I've always been an outdoorsy type. When I was a teen, they called me the nature nut." And the nut has stuck with her passion, working for Parks Canada and BC Parks before starting her own interpretive service and nature tours.

At a Glance

Naturalist Roseanne Van Ee offers a selection of tours that concentrate on different areas of interest and hiking ability. Options include the mountain wildflowers tour as well as walks for birders, history buffs and other crazies like me who want to learn about bears. Visit www.outdoordiscoveries.com for more details. To book a tour, click on Summer at www.skisilverstar.com and follow the links.

Wild strawberries.

Naturalist Roseanne Van Ee.

Roseanne gathers our little group at the summit lookout. The August sun flays every detail of the landscape with its harsh glare. In the valley it's blistering, but at 1,884 metres, I feel a high-altitude chill as she describes the glacial forces that shaped the Okanagan. On a clear day, the panorama extends from New Denver to Revelstoke taking in the Monashee, Valhalla, Selkirk and Bugaboo ranges. It's an incredibly diverse collection of ecosystems including the transition from the hottest and driest in Canada to the second wettest—the interior rain forest.

Standing here, it's easy to see why native people climbed to this peak each spring to map out their hunting plans for the season. As Roseanne describes their annual routines, she dips into her backpack like a magician delving into the magic hat and whips out a tightly woven cedar basket. Historic photographs follow. "I've worked with the Okanagan people and elders," she says, "and they've passed on a lot of knowledge."

Down the trail, she stops to cut a stalk of cow parsnip (also known as Indian rhubarb) and peels back the outer layer. The celery-like stalk, which she passes around for us to taste (bland and faintly soapy), was once a staple food for First Nations people.

Roseanne's hands-on blend of history and nature extends to every part of the tour. At the site of the Silver Queen Mine, another excursion into the backpack produces more historic photos and a lump of fool's gold as she recounts the story of nearby O'Keefe Ranch. At a tumble-down log cabin we learn about the transition from miner's camp to ski resort. And as we descend the mountain trail, a mere thread amid the profusion of shin-high grasses and flowers—Indian paintbrush (spectacular in shades of red through orange) and fireweed (burning up the hillsides in great swaths of gently swaying fuchsia)—she tells us it's okay to pick the berries but not the wildflowers.

With Roseanne, no two tours are alike. She says she's constantly adapting to the unexpected, like suddenly coming upon a bear digging a hole. "I had to get everybody to stop, and back up—very carefully."

No kidding. (Wish I'd been in that group.)

Meadows in the Sky Parkway

THE FLOWER SHOW STARTS the minute we pull off the Trans-Canada Highway and pass through the Mount Revelstoke National Park gate. With July giving way to August, the season is nearing its peak. Bruce and I are making the day trip from the Okanagan specifically to take in the sights along the twenty-six kilometre paved road whose switchbacks lead right to the summit. This is the only place in the national park system where you can drive a private vehicle in such comfort to a mountaintop.

We dawdle through a green bower of cedar and hemlock, walls of dense vegetation crowding the blacktop and screening the sun. Within the park, the old growth interior rainforest of the Columbia Mountains is protected, but beyond its borders, this unique ecosystem is rapidly disappearing.

The road climbs steadily from an elevation of 470 metres at kilometre-zero to 1,500 metres at Balsam Lake, winding upward through mid-level zones of spruce and fir to the subalpine flower meadows. Vivid red Indian paintbrush, distinct from the orangey shades we're used to in the Okanagan, lines the ditches.

When we pull over for a view-stop at the first lookout, the entire town of Revelstoke presents itself in a neat grid bordering the blue ribbon of the Columbia River. Across the valley, peaks in the Monashee Range still wear the last of their winter toques, a reminder of just how much white stuff falls in these mountains—up to eighteen metres a year.

At a Glance

Meadows in the Sky Parkway is located in Mount Revelstoke National Park. At the summit, stay on the marked trails. Subalpine vegetation is very fragile. In an area with such a short growing season, any damage to plants is serious. And don't pick the flowers, please leave them for the next guy to enjoy. The parkway is a narrow mountain road. Trailers and motor coaches are not allowed. If you're dragging a trailer, park it in the designated area, half-a-kilometre from the Trans-Canada Highway interchange. National Park fees apply with both day and seasonal rates available. Visit www.pc.gc.ca for details.

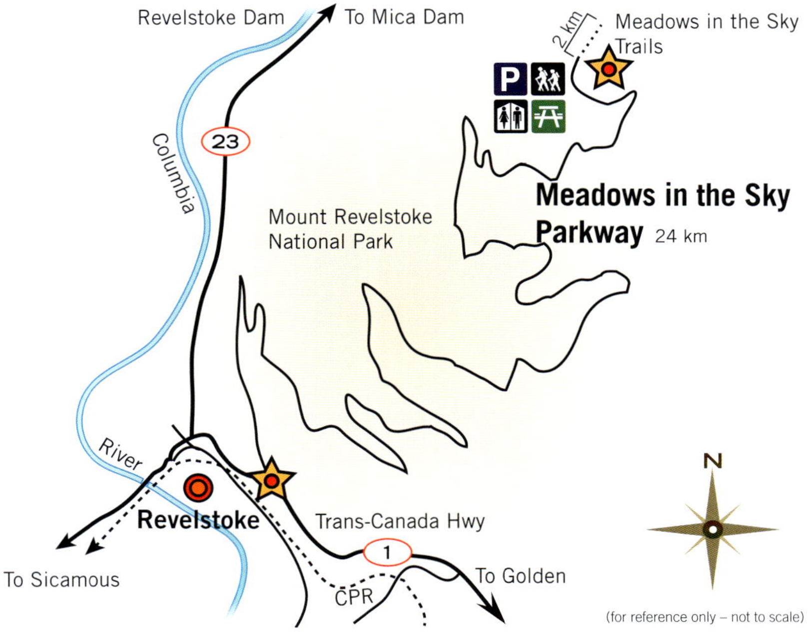

That snowfall and near vertical terrain make Mount Revelstoke the ideal location for a natural ski jump. International competitions were held here almost every year between 1915 and 1971. You can hike from the parkway to the Nels Nelsen Historic Ski Jump exhibit, but we've left our visit a little late in the day and have to press on for the summit.

A blue grouse hen strolls onto the road and pauses to watch us pass. Makes me wonder if local wildlife regards the stream of vehicles as a daily parade mounted by thoughtful humans for their amusement.

For our amusement, nature has mounted a constantly evolving display. Higher up, patches of lupines appear—deep violet—sometimes in exclusive beds, sometimes mixed with that strikingly red paintbrush or sunny yellow flowers I can't name. No pastels in this world. Every blossom, leaf and needle fairly vibrates with colour. Maybe it's because the growing season is so short, the conditions so harsh. When they put on their summer finery, these plants have to go all out.

It's hard to believe that such a beautiful place harbours the memory of a disturbing and dark bit of Canadian history—an episode I'd never even heard of before browsing the National Park website.

Citizens of Revelstoke have always enjoyed a love affair with their mountain. The City of Revelstoke undertook to drive the first trail to the summit in 1908 and lobbying by local residents was directly responsible for creation of the national park in 1914. Pressure to turn the trail into a road was ongoing. Construction began in 1911 … and then that dark stain appeared.

During the First World War, feeling against "enemy aliens" ran high. Invoking a clause of the War Measures Act, the government created Canada's first internment camps at twenty-four different sites across the country. Four of the camps were set up in the mountain parks: Banff, Jasper, Yoho and Mount Revelstoke.

Meadows in the Sky Parkway provides close access to summit trails in Mount Revelstoke National Park.

Approximately eight thousand people were imprisoned. Most were Ukrainians who had come here for jobs in railway construction, mining and forestry, from regions that were then ruled by the Austro-Hungarian Empire. Since they carried Austrian passports, or in some cases, no papers at all, they were rounded up and detained. Some were still in custody in the late spring of 1920, a year-and-a-half after the armistice was signed. No wonder our history books have been shy about revealing this chapter in our past.

Flash back to the citizens of Revelstoke, some of whom knew a good thing when they saw it. As long as the "aliens" where being held on their doorstep, they might as well be put to work to complete the summit road. And the Dominion Parks Commissioner agreed. As it happened, the scheme was short-lived, with the Mount Revelstoke camp only operating from September 6 to December 20, 1915. Horrific weather conditions forced the internees to spend their time clearing snow and cutting firewood rather than building the road and the two hundred and twenty-five detainees were moved to Camp Otter in Yoho. The road wasn't finally completed until 1927. An interpretive sign now records the story.

Sobering thoughts for a brilliant summer afternoon, and while we can't change the past, we need to be aware of it—and learn from it.

At Balsam Lake, two kilometres short of the summit, we reach the parking lot—and things get exciting. Living in the Okanagan (a virtually mosquito-free Utopia), we tend to forget about flying villains. But up where the summer is short and the food supply limited, mossies are a force to be reckoned with. They attack in squadrons, buzzing in from every direction the moment the car door opens.

It's not that we lack resources. There's always a bottle of Deet in my backpack. But the little blighters catch us completely by surprise—and my pack is in the trunk. It's astonishing how the distance between the passenger door and the rear of a tiny car can expand, apparently in direct proportion to the amount of blood being sucked from your quivering flesh. I eventually root the killer spray from the deepest recesses of my bag and we douse each other sufficiently to deter even the most voracious attackers (probably causing permanent neurological damage). Checking out the hiking options, we decide to wimp out (weakened by blood loss), take the park shuttle to the summit and leg it back down.

Scratching absently, we jump on the minibus and minutes later are walking in meadows crowded, bursting with blossoms. We skirt a mirror-surfaced pond that doubles the images of skeletal high-altitude trees, riotous flowers and one stubborn patch of snow, and follow the paved path to a viewpoint overlooking the Columbia as it flows south from the Big Bend.

That is as far as a pair of pic-addicted photogs made it together. Each of us follows our own lens—Bruce wandering the first section of the relatively flat trail toward Eva Lake, me puffing the short, sharp climb to an historic fire tower.

Eventually our paths reconnect and together we work our way back to the car. The light is just starting to slant through the trees, casting barcode shadows as we tackle the switchbacks in reverse. We're rounding one of the last bends when the long, dark shape of a marten materialized from the undergrowth and, almost as suddenly, vanishes—one last gift from the mountain.

Historic fire spotting tower on Mount Revelstoke.

Desert Centre Osoyoos boardwalk. Facing page: Yellow bellied marmot at Allan Brooks Nature Centre.

Chapter 5

Eco Friendly

"We have not inherited the earth from our fathers,
We are borrowing it from our children."

Esther R. Brown

THE OKANAGAN VALLEY PRESENTS one of the most diverse collection of ecosystems in Canada. It also hosts some of the most threatened. In my quest to learn more about the fragile and endangered ecosystems around me, hopeful that we can preserve something of what remains, a couple of themes have emerged—fire and rattlers. Apparently I'm fixated on both, which makes for some unique adventures.

Garnet Fire Interpretive Site

"ONLY YOU CAN PREVENT FOREST FIRES!"

Not a boomer among us would fail to recognize Smokey the Bear's one great line. Every summer he pointed his finger from our black and white TV screens. His face stared out of posters at every campsite and park. Commercials bombarded us with images of terrified Bambies fleeing a relentless inferno. We were taught one immutable truth—forest fires are bad!

Ooops . . .

Echo boomers (kids of the millennial generation) are learning a different truth. In fact, they're relearning what the Okanagan First Nations always knew. Forest fires are a natural event here. They change and rejuvenate forest ecosystems, clear out disease and weeds, fertilize the soil and create new habitats that foster biodiversity.

Before European contact changed their way of life, the Okanagan Peoples left wildfires to burn and sometimes even lit their own controlled fires to keep habitats healthy. Specific individuals were responsible for setting strip fires up mountainsides as a method of hunting deer and other game. A resulting side benefit was the increased growth of shrubs and berries used by both animals and people. In late summer and fall they moved their encampments to avoid fire prone areas.

Unfortunately, we can't pick up our homes to get out of harm's way. And with constantly increasing development in the wilderness/urban interface (areas close to forests and grasslands with natural wildfire cycles), what's good for the forest isn't always good for the people living near it. Just ask the three thousand Penticton residents who were evacuated during the 1994 Garnet Fire that burned for thirty days before being declared controlled—that's controlled—not out. It scorched fifty-five hundred hectares of canyons and mountainside east of the city and took out eighteen homes.

At a Glance

To reach the Garnet Fire Interpretive Site follow Carmi Avenue east from Main Street in Penticton. Turn right on Beaverdell Road and keep going until you see the signs.

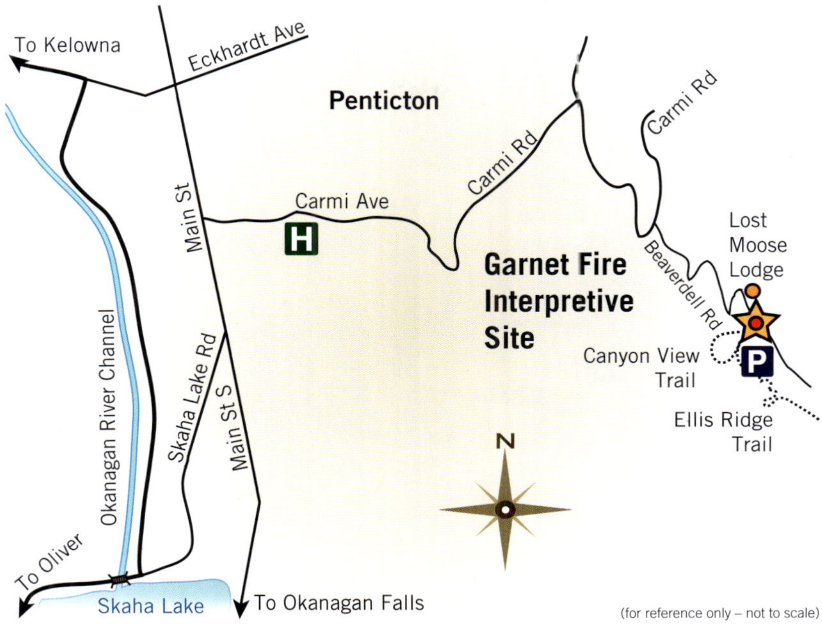

But, like the forest, people recover. Take a drive up Carmi Avenue today and you'll find new homes standing amidst the blackened tree skeletons and nature's renewal in high gear. The Ministry of Forests seized on the opportunity presented by a readily accessible fire zone and developed the Garnet Fire Interpretive Site. A kiosk at the parking/picnic area details the local burn history, explains fire ecology and maps out the two trails. Ellis Ridge is the more challenging of the pair and leads to a popular mountain bike trail. Canyon View is a fairly level kilometre-and-a-half loop. Bruce and I take the easy route.

Topping the slight rise where the trails fork, a mule deer freezes us in our tracks as she springs through a stand of ponderosas to a nearby rock outcrop. She turns and makes eye contact, giving us a moment to commune before she moves on—obviously Bambie's cousins know the ropes in fire country. Along with birds and other large mammals, deer usually smell smoke early enough to get out of harm's way. Smaller critters like marmots, hares, chipmunks and snakes hide underground or escape the heat deep in rocky crevices.

Garnet Fire Interpretive Site, Penticton.

Before Smokey's day, fire swept the forest floor every ten to fifteen years, cleaning up the dead and diseased plants and nourishing the soil with a layer of mineral-rich ash. Everything that lives here is well adapted to the burning cycle. Thick bark protects older ponderosa pines and Douglas firs while many of the younger, closely spaced trees succumb to nature's own thinning process. After a fire, Saskatoon and Ceanothus bushes regenerate from their stems. Bunchgrass thrives on ash soil and its deep root balls have no trouble surviving surface fires. Fireweed seeds, floating in on the wind, are among the first signs of rebirth in burn areas. In the natural system, truly destructive crown fires happened only once in a century or more.

Hiking the canyon trail we can see the results of evolving forest management practices. The first half runs through a thirty-metre wide firebreak where trees were pruned two to three metres up. It was created in 1982 to keep fires on the forest floor and the ponderosas that survived in this area prove it was a good idea. Further along only a few black snags mark the place where a dense stand of Douglas firs former-ly grew. Close spacing allowed the fire to spread from branch to branch. But even these skeletons have their place in the fire ecology. Known as wildlife trees, they now support a host of animals by providing food, storage spaces, perches and shelter.

Mice and voles nest in the fallen branches and trunks. Frogs and the like seek out the moist shade beneath them Insects that invade dead and dying trees attract woodpeckers, sapsuckers and songbirds. The cavities they create while drilling for lunch eventually make nice nesting spaces for bats and owls and warehouses for martens, squir-rels and chipmunks.

Two lookouts on the circuit give us a macro perspective. Along with an eagle's eye view of Penticton and panorama of the whole valley from Mount Kobau to Peachland, we see the Garnet Fire's erratic track. The patchy landscape, created when shifting winds backed the fire and left healthy clusters of trees amid the general devastation, offers a range of habitats and increased biodiversity.

When we first hiked the trail in 2003 the regeneration was remark-able, both for the forest and for the people who call the area home. Winged and four-footed creatures aren't the only ones who know how to make use of what the fire left.

A few hundred metres from the trailhead, the Lost Moose Lodge was constructed almost entirely from burnt trees salvaged from the property—two hundred and seventy-one in all. The biggest now forms a massive one-piece bar with enough left over to make tabletops and a bench at the barbecue hut. The party line is that this giant was one hundred and twenty-eight years old. We try to confirm this ourselves by counting the rings in our table over lunch one day. Despite a glass or two of the Okanagan's finest fruit of the vine and carefully exclud-ing water rings, we come pretty close.

This is one of the best parts of visiting the Garnet site (no, not ring counting, although that can be diverting). I'm talking about treating yourself to an outdoor-grilled burger (or salmon or chicken). The view from the Lost Moose deck is unbelievable and for non-hikers it pro-vides a terrific armchair look at Okanagan fire ecology in action.

Okanagan Mountain Park Fire Tour

"I'VE SPENT TWENTY YEARS LOOKING DOWN AT THE ROCKS," says exploration geologist Steve Noakes from behind the wheel of his four-by-four. "Now I'm looking up at the trees." Ironically, most of the trees are blackened skeletons. We're on Gillard Creek Forest Service Road climbing into the aftermath of the 2003 Okanagan Mountain Park Fire.

Steve, whose prospecting career ranged from Chile to the Yukon, had been operating backcountry tours from Kelowna. The fire really put a dent in his summer business, but he quickly recognized that it also presented an unusual learning opportunity and set about organizing tours into the area.

We aren't long on the road when I begin to see the same bizarre pattern in the forest as I'd witnessed while covering the story of the fire-ravaged subdivisions in the city. Islands of green, dotted with butter-yellow aspens, somehow stand untouched amid great swaths of monochrome moonscape where nothing remains but black spikes, stark against the ash-gray, rock-strewn earth. Looking more closely, though, I realize that these islands didn't actually escape the burn. It's just that new grass is already growing so thickly that I have to look hard to see the scorch-marks where ground-fire swept through. That kind of wildfire is a natural event in the Okanagan.

"Smokey the Bear was wrong," says Steve. When it comes to fire, "our human sense of esthetics collides with nature . . . something that looks bad to us isn't necessarily bad at all." He cites a study that examined the cross-section of a three-hundred-year-old ponderosa pine. The tree showed traces of fire every seven years—until fifty years ago. That's when Smokey started warning us about forest fires … and the danger started to grow.

In the natural system, destructive crown fires happened only once

At a Glance

Regrettably, Steve Noakes is no longer conducting his Geoqwest Excursions (something about government red tape) and the Okanagan eco-tourism experience is poorer as a result.

in a century or more. But decades of prevention have changed the forest, allowing "fuel" to build to such levels that each outbreak has the potential to turn into a monster like the Okanagan Mountain Park Fire that caused the evacuation of over thirty-three thousand people, consumed over twenty-five thousand hectares of forest and destroyed two hundred and thirty-eight homes. Thanks, Smokey.

Left on its own, everything that lives in the Okanagan is well adapted to the burning cycle. Before Smokey's day, regular fires cleaned up the windfalls and thinned out many of the younger, closely spaced firs. Ponderosas dominated the area and bunch grass flourished. But without the natural fires, Douglas firs have taken over.

The result is obvious as we drive through a forest of scorched trunks standing as thick as the hairs on a dog's back. We stop in the midst of Armageddon and climb out for a look. The air smells of stale smoke and touching the earth is like stirring your fingers through an old campfire pit. I'm struck by the utter silence. In the light breeze, there isn't a leaf to stir.

Steve warns me to stay on the road as he walks carefully into the "bush." He's explaining the dangers of these incinerated areas when—whoomph—my guide disappears. Well, his legs are gone and he's suddenly half-a-metre shorter.

"See what I mean," he says, gingerly pulling one leg free of the hole he's dropped into. It's like watching a kid wade through heavy snow as he plunges knee-deep into the ash with each step. Before he finds solid footing, Steve has opened up a cavern nearly two metres wide.

That's what happens when fire burns down into the tree roots. It can spread far out under what appears to be solid ground. Clear-cuts are particularly bad because the stumps burn away and then the fire tunnels. Areas like that won't be safe until after a heavy snow-load settles the earth. Falling trees are another hazard. I stoop down to photograph the hole burned into the base of one apparently solid tree-trunk. With such weakness at ground level, it won't take much of a wind to topple.

Back in the four-by-four, we climb the ridge beside the hydro tower line and I get a good sense of how fireguards work. Turn one way and the landscape looks like the black and white photo of a First World War battlefield. Look the other, and it's a Group of Seven painting.

Steve Noakes drops through surface crust into holes left when tree roots burned underground.

Along the way we meet two workers unloading an ATV-mounted seeder from the back of a pickup. Because I'm curious, they pull a tag off one of the bags piled alongside and I see that they're spreading a cocktail of nine different seeds including fescue, wheatgrass, timothy and clover. Where possible they'll stick with the ATV, but tough terrain will force them to go on foot and carry backpacks. Reclamation crews are working all over the mountain—downing danger trees, spreading straw to stabilize the soil and prevent creeks from silting up and laying logs across steep fire guards to slow erosion. For about a year, before the wood dries out and cracks, timber that isn't too badly burned can still be harvested.

I'm surprised to learn that the great red swaths of fire retardant, dropped by choppers and planes during the air assault, will also help in the renewal. Fire retardant is made of ammonium nitrate—it's fertilizer.

And Mother Nature is doing her magic. Even as the fire burned, she was laying the groundwork for regeneration. Being a geologist, Steve can't resist the opportunity to demonstrate how she creates new soil.

"It's all a dynamic process, all linked together," he says, squatting beside a boulder and fingering the shards of rock lying loose on its surface. "Just add a few hundred degrees Celsius." I follow his lead and easily break a chunk of granite with my bare hands, just like snapping a carrot stick. The process is called exfoliation—think Mother Nature getting a facial.

During the fire, heat fractures the rock and layers peel off. It also leaves cracks on the surface of the boulder where water can seep in. Over time, freezing and thawing cause more shards to slough away and eventually these pieces break down into soil.

Clumps of fern have already sprouted beneath the hydro towers and shoots of green are beginning to relieve the dull gray burn areas where aspens grew. While these trees are thin-barked and easily destroyed, they're also among the first to return because they regenerate from runners sent up from their roots. Wherever the fire didn't burn too deep, they're good to go.

Passing through the worst areas, it's hard to imagine any living creature surviving the blaze. But even burned trees have their place in the fire ecology. Known as wildlife trees, they will soon support a host of animals by providing food, storage spaces, perches and shelter. Life goes on. Steve points out a meadow where, the day before, he'd seen a herd of whitetail deer, and further along a rocky outcrop he spotted a bobcat. I'm not so lucky. A couple of grouse scooting off the road are all I see.

At the summit we skirt the shores of Lebanon Lake, where new scars mark hastily cleared roads for tanker trucks, and turn onto the old Kettle Valley Railway bed—the KVR Trail. From here, the run to Chute Lake only takes about twenty minutes. Along the way I'm treated to another happy side effect of the fire. Before, cycling along here was like riding in a tunnel, running alternately through rock cuts and a thick forest screen. Now, amazing views open up with each new turn in the trail. At one point, we stop for a look at the three peaks of Okanagan Mountain Park. At another, we can see all the way from Rimrock north toward Fintry.

When we reached Chute Lake Resort, I'm delighted to see the old landmark unscathed and as busy as it was when Bruce and I visited in the spring. One more sign of life moving on.

Rock exfoliation caused by very hot fires starts the process of creating new soil

Allan Brooks Nature Centre

"HEY, YOU WANT TO SEE SOMETHING NEAT?"

I turned from the entrance to the Allan Brooks Nature Centre to where a teenaged girl was beckoning from the shrubbery. She waved for me to join the knot of hunched figures peering intently at an ordinary looking bush. "It's moving," said someone. I hurried over. The group parted like the Red Sea and I joined a ragged circle staring into the choke cherries.

Aha! A fat green caterpillar, as long as the first two segments of my index finger, raised its head. The excited observers, who I learned were volunteers, told me all about the little critter, which was actually the larva stage of the western tiger swallowtail butterfly. Seeing it was a highlight of my visit the summer the centre opened.

A decade later, much has changed—and much hasn't. The Allan Brooks Nature Centre occupies the old Environment Canada weather station on Mission Hill south of Vernon. It stands as an isolated island in an open expanse of grassland known as The Commonage.

Founders of the centre had the vision of increasing public awareness and actually doing something to protect and reclaim the badly endangered grassland ecosystem. You get a better idea of just what's at stake in the Habitat Room where brilliantly coloured murals painted by local artist Andrea Toth, with bird and animal illustrations by Ginny Hall, depict four local ecosystems—grasslands, wetlands, ponderosa pine forests and mountains, specifically Silver Star.

In the Discovery Room, exhibits change every few years. Currently it's all about raptors. "Kids love Harry Potter's owl," says centre manager Mary Jong, pointing out the snowy bird in a glass case.

At a Glance

The Allan Brooks Nature Centre offers a hands-on learning experience (that's actually fun) with indoor exhibits, 360-degree viewpoints, signage interpreting local geography and ecology and a four hundred-metre grasslands walking trail. Located at 250 Allan Brooks Way in Vernon, the centre is open Tuesday to Sunday from May 1 to mid-October. Get details at www.abnc.ca.

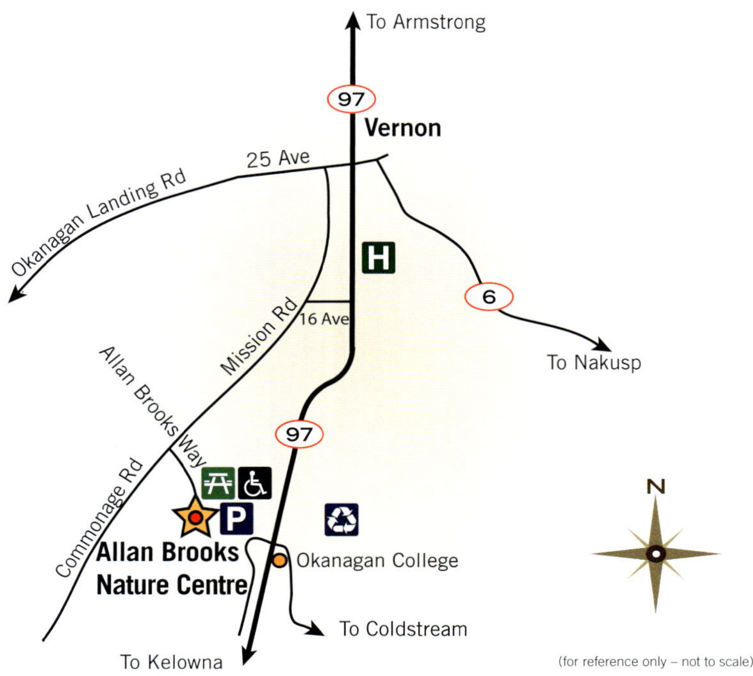

But I'm more knocked out by the juvenile bald eagle, with a wingspan as wide as my arms can reach, that seems to be flying in through the corner windows. A peregrine falcon is posed over its fallen prey while a hawk wings overhead.

Discovery is hands-on in this room. "We encourage people to spend as much time as they want to," says Jane, a volunteer who helps kids spot the queen bee in the glass-walled hive or get an insect's-eye view of the world through a multi-facetted viewer. She hands the little gizmo to Kaitlyn, a first-time visitor from Slave Lake, Alberta, who peers through the lens at her brother and grandmother. They're busy studying the array of bird's nests in a drawer. "Awesome," she says. "It's great to have something interesting to do."

The centre commands a spectacular view. I stand at the lookout and do a three-sixty—taking in Predator Ridge; Okanagan Lake; the city, with Swan Lake in the distance; Silver Star Mountain, Vernon Hill, Middleton Mountain, the Rimrocks, the Coldstream Valley stretching toward the white-tipped Monashees; and Kalamalka

I shot this western tiger swallowtail butterfly larva just a few centimetres from the egg below.

Swallowtail butterflies lay their eggs on choke cherry leaves at the entrance to the Allan Brooks Nature Centre.

Centre manager Mary Jong in the Habitat Room.

Sharp beaks rule in the Raptors of the Okanagan exhibit.

The Grasslands Trail showcases a seriously endangered ecosystem.

Lake—sapphire, jade or emerald—depending on her mood. Excellent signage interprets the landscape beginning with the fault in the Earth's crust that led to the formation of the Okanagan Valley about fifty million years ago.

I spot the family from Slave Lake on the Grasslands Trail below and follow. It's an easy walk, just four hundred metres, through habitat that's only found at low elevations in the hot, dry valleys of the BC Interior. If I'd been strolling this hillside a couple of hundred years ago, I'd have been wading through swaying grasses in a landscape splashed like a painter's palette with the yellows, blues and reds of wildflowers. This fragile ecosystem is seriously threatened, but efforts are under way to turn back the clock.

Burrowing owls are gone, but a badger family moved in for a time in the summer of 2010, attracted by the prospect of a meal in Marmot City on the trail. Badgers love to eat the little ones. When I visited in August, the badgers had left, but I met a young marmot. Bluebirds nest in houses installed on fence posts and spadefoot toads have returned to the pond. Overhead a turkey vulture rides the thermals and a red-tailed hawk dives for a mouse in the grasses.

"You want to see something," Mary asks, leading me to the now tall choke cherry bushes. She pulls aside a branch and points to a tiny round ball. "That's a swallowtail egg," she says. "And over here, is a larva." Sure enough, there is another of the fat green creatures I saw that first day. .

I believe that Major Allan C. Brooks, the centre's namesake, would be very pleased—not with the damage humans have done since he lived in the Okanagan Landing area in the early 20th century—but with the hard work that volunteers are putting into reclamation.

The Commonage was one of his favourite birdwatching venues and forms the background for many of his pictures. His work was featured in publications like National Geographic Magazine and Robert Bateman says that Brooks' paintings inspired him during his own formative years as a wildlife artist. A collection of Brooks' work is displayed at the Vernon Museum. But to get a real sense of what he was all about, you need to walk a mile in his shoes—and the nature centre is the place to do it.

California bighorn sheep wearing a radio collar.

Spadefoot toads are trying to make a comeback.

Desert Centre boardwalk provides access without disturbing the endangered antelope brush ecosystem.

Desert Centre Osoyoos

IT WON'T CONJURE IMAGES OF LAWRENCE OF ARABIA—nor will it remind you of Tucson or Baja. Yet the South Okanagan does encompass an arid desert. This is the northern outpost of the Great Basin Desert—that's right, the Great Basin, not the Sonoran Desert, although that's a common local misnomer.

Whatever you call it, this is one of the most special and most endangered ecosystems in North America, home to over one hundred rare plants and three hundred rare invertebrates. Through the decades, ranching, orchards and urban sprawl have steadily consumed the fragile antelope brush ecosystem. Tragically, only about nine per cent of the desert habitat remains undisturbed. Many residents like the burrowing owl, spadefoot toad, tiger salamander and Mariposa lily are either threatened or endangered.

This ecological crisis galvanized a group of local residents to form the Osoyoos Desert Society. Headed by the visionary Ruth Schiller, they set about finding a way to save at least a representative area. It took eight years, but on July 2, 1999, the Desert Centre officially opened.

The first season I take a look, lured by an intriguing brochure. Eco-tourism is in its infancy and I'm very curious to see what's shaping up. Clearly the project is still a work in progress. Tours conducted by knowledgeable and enthusiastic guides are necessarily short. The centrepiece boardwalk that will eventually make a one-and-three-quarter-kilometre loop through the 26.8-hectare site (protecting the fragile environment from tromping tourist feet) is only a couple of hundred metres long.

We make stops at four kiosks (slated to be outfitted with interpretive signage) and get down on our hands and knees to peer through the cracks between the planks in the boardwalk. Our guide assures us

At a Glance

The Desert Centre Osoyoos is located four kilometres north of Osoyoos, west of Hwy 97 on Road 146. Open daily, late April to early-October, look for details on hours and seasonal events (including the annual Romancing the Desert Gala) at www.desert.org.

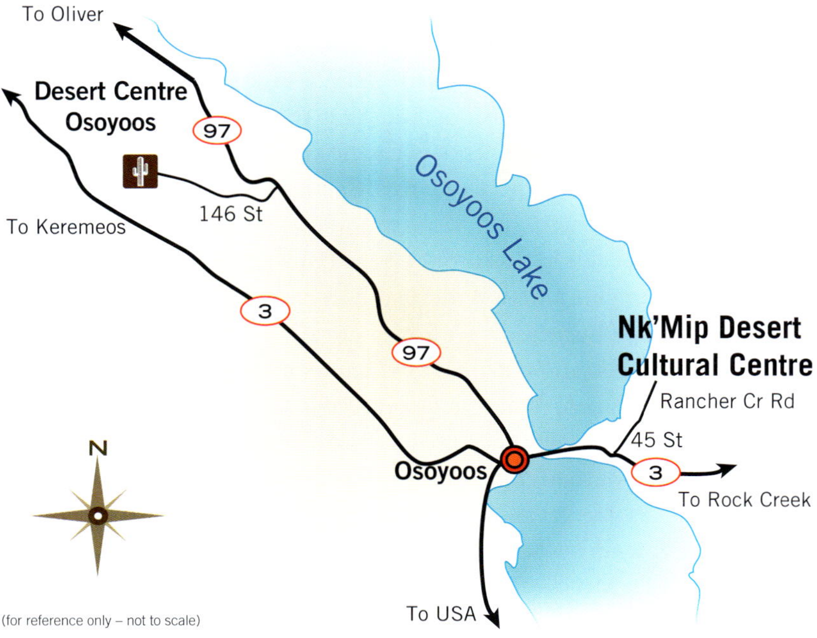

that a rattler is sheltering from the sun right beneath. (*Yes!*)

I *want* to see a rattler in the wild—with certain conditions. Something in a nice controlled encounter where my feet, hands and bum are well out of striking range seems appropriate. Something involving a nice knowledgeable naturalist and a two-inch thick barrier seems ideal. We don't see the snake.

I do, however, learn that the Desert Centre occupies a plot of land once used for cattle ranching. Ironically, while grazing is a major cause of damage to fragile grasslands, in this case it was actually somewhat beneficial. Ranching kept the land from being totally changed as it would have been if planted to orchards or carved up for a subdivision. But it suffered from other problems such as the invasion of native plant-killers like knapweed. As part of an ecological restoration research project, we can see sheets of plastic spread out to kill the killers and new garden plots to propagate native species.

We gather around another experiment that's making good use of a holdover from ranching days—a former water trough now provides breeding habitat for spadefoot toads. It's encouraging to hear that badgers are also making a comeback and with them, there's hope for the reintroduction of burrowing owls who nest in their holes.

When I return to the Desert Centre a year later, things have noticeably progressed. Families of mountain bluebirds are nesting in newly installed boxes. The boardwalk is more than half finished; signage has appeared in the first of the interpretive kiosks and the research projects are in full swing. Best of all, I stumble on a special tour being conducted by Dr. Geoffrey Scudder, head of the society's ad hoc science committee. I tag along.

Sporting a red plaid shirt and safari hat, the world famous entomologist makes a stab at sharing his passion for bugs. Carefully stepping off the boardwalk, he retrieves a nearby hidden trap—very high-tech.

"Are you all familiar with black widows?" he asks, thrusting forward a disposable beer cup. Apparently clever spiders like to build their webs across the top of the traps and dine on insects as they enter. Okay, that's cool. I've never seen a black widow before—but still no rattler.

So I keep going back. Now the boardwalk is complete, there's a new spadefoot toad pond and a string of bat boxes. Spring is my favourite time. It's not so blistering hot and while the antelope brush has already flowered, bitterroot blooms in late May followed by prickly-pear cactus and, later in June, the mariposa lilies. Seeing the desert in full flower is really something—but still no rattler.

Like most rattle snakes in the South Okanagan, this guy was very hard to spot as it found shade and seclusion under the antelope brush. I finally got my first sighting at the Nk'Mip Desesrt Cultural Centre.

Nk'Mip Desert Cultural Centre

WHY DID THE BIOLOGIST PAINT the rattler's tail yellow?

As Bruce and I approach the trailer that served as visitor centre before the stunning new digs at Nk'Mip opened in 2006, we aren't expecting a lesson in reptile tail painting. But when the ticket seller mentions that a rattler identification session is under way; we rush to take a look.

Not that I'm crazy about snakes. Actually, I hate snakes. No, I mean, I *really* hate snakes. When my daughter was small, I made a super-human effort to feign herpetological appreciation (pretty fancy, huh? That's pseudo-Greek for reptile liking). But the little vixen saw right through my ruse and now she hates them even more than I do. Still, I have to admit to a nagging fascination—especially with the lethal varieties. Maybe it's some sort of partially suppressed Eve-transference disorder—ETD? Back to the point.

Despite my aversion, I want to see a rattler. After all, they are an important component of the Okanagan pocket desert ecosystem. But the venomous vipers are getting awfully scarce. Loss of habitat and relentless hunting have put them on the blue list as a threatened species. My chances of spotting one in the wild are about as good as getting the definitive word on where Wayne Gretzke is building his Okanagan getaway (or is that just a rumour?). Back to the point.

I finally find my rattler submitting to the tender ministrations of a couple of otherwise sensible-looking people. Biologist Mike Sarell grips the snake carefully (no kidding), directly behind the head and near the

At a Glance

The Nk'Mip Desert Cultural Centre protects twenty hectares of the highly endangered Okanagan desert environment. Developed by the Osoyoos Indian Band, the outstanding interpretive centre hosts both ecological and cultural experiences. (Read about the cultural side in chapter 8). Exhibits and demonstrations focus on the flora and fauna of the desert, especially the snakes, while self-guided walking trails with excellent signage make it easy to explore the natural setting first hand. Open from May through mid-September. See map on page 108. For seasonal hours, rates and schedule of daily tours and demonstrations, visit www.nkmipdesert.com.

Deer roam freely among the interpretive displays at the Nk'Mip Desert Cultural Centre.

row of rattle segments on its tail where research assistant and interpreter Sherry Linn is applying yellow paint. Bizarre.

But what surprises me almost as much as this insane tableau is the
rattler's size. At sixty-eight centimetres (I know, because I watched the
snake charmers wield a tape measure) and not much bigger around
than my big toe, this is not the fearsome reptile of my nightmares.
Mike says this fella is about average. These days, few live long or well
enough to grow bigger. To get its weight, he drops the rattler into a
high-tech snake bag (read pillowcase) and hangs the lot from a fish
scale.

When all the measurements are recorded Mike invites us to join
the release party. Our small convoy marches along a gravel path into
the twenty-hectare area protected by the Osoyoos Indian Band as part
of the Nk'Mip site. Knee-high sage, rabbit brush and antelope brush
paint multi-hued green abstracts on the dry slope. Pink and white
long-leafed phlox splashes the background and red-barked ponderosa
pines climb the rocky ridge beyond. The scent of sage hangs heavy in
the gathering heat beneath a cloudless blue sky.

Mike carries three captives in his high-tech reptile transporter

Biologist Kyle Horner tries to locate Newman the rattler by tracking the snake's radio transmitter.

(latch-topped kitchen garbage can). I scribble notes while interpreter and research assistant, Shelley Witzky, uses a GPS to find the precise location. She explains that rattlers are very territorial and need to be returned to the same area where they were captured.

All snakes studied in the joint Osoyoos Indian Band/Canadian Wildlife Service research program are tagged with a microchip so they can be studied in their natural environment. A small number are fitted with a radio transmitter to track their movements for two years (until they shed their skin along with the transmitter). The painted tails alert researchers to snakes that have previously been tagged so they aren't captured again.

When Shelley locates the release point, Mike shows us a safe spot to stand. Moment of truth—here at last is my chance to see a rattler in the wild. I step behind Bruce.

Mike lays the container on its side and flips the latches. The inmates don't hesitate. There's barely time to focus a shot (okay, so photo-greed trumps reptile phobia) before the rattlers' camouflage makes them all but invisible as they slide away into the brush. First hand evidence that these are actually shy and elusive creatures.

"If you see one," says Mike, "you've probably passed ten." He suggests spring and fall as the best times for sightings when the snakes are on the move to or from their winter dens. In summer they're particularly inactive during the day, sheltering close to the stems of bushes and doing everything they can to avoid human contact.

I see how close to invisible they can make themselves when I'm invited for another visit in June 2006, just before the grand opening of the new centre. Biologist Kyle Horner takes a small group of journalists along on his daily trek into the nature preserve to see which rattlers he can find. He's particularly keen to track down Newman, one of the select critters fitted with a radio transmitter. Even armed with a techno-gizmo that guides us to within a few metres, Newman is incredibly hard to find.

Kyle calls out his readings as he zigzags a search pattern. "Warm, warmer—no, getting colder—oh, hot, hotter, hotter!"

"Stay on the path," he warns (no argument here) and begins poking around in the brush with his long snake stick. It still takes several minutes to finally locate Newman, curled into a tight knot against the thick stem of an antelope bush. He lies motionless, his colour and markings blending so perfectly with the dusty soil and dry wood that a walker casually passing just a metre away would never see him.

So the best chance for sighting these denizens of the desert is actually back at the centre. Western rattlers that are briefly captured for research hang out in Critter Corner (nice solid glass walls). And you can catch biologists or interpreters hosting demonstrations, including the tail-painting thing, in the outdoor Living Lands Gallery.

By the way—the biologist painted the rattler's tail yellow, because blue and red were already taken.

Orchard near Oliver. Facing Page: Kelowna Land & Orchard Company.

Chapter 6

Down on the Farm

APPLES HOLD A DEEP PSYCHOLOGICAL ATTACHMENT
for me. When I was a kid I spent every weekend on my grandparent's
small farm near Kitchener, Ontario. The orchard was a place of unbridled
imagination, the site of countless adventures in which I played all the
roles. As I grew older, my connection with the apples marked important
rights of passage in my life. Around age six I was allowed to help pick,
working the lower branches and taking great care not to break off the
stems. A year or two later, I graduated to climbing the tall ladders and
when I was at last entrusted with manning the roadside stand—serving
customers and making change—I had arrived. Spring blossoms and
the smell of ripening apples transport me to a very happy place, so the
orchards and farm markets of the Okanagan are more than special to me.

Davison Orchards

THE AVERAGE APPLE HARVESTER hand picks enough fruit every day to fill four of those big red bins we see all around the valley in the autumn. At over three hundred and sixty kilograms each, that amounts to something like 1.5 tonnes of apples—per picker.

I learned this amazing apple fact when I first went walk-about at Davison Orchards in 2000. This is also when I met Tamra Davison, an Energizer-bunny of a woman who pops up here and there around the family-run complex offering service and doling out info bits.

She says the self-guided tour is a great hit with visitors who learn a little about farming and the history of the area on their own. But I'm a sucker for the Johnny Popper tour (even with the added challenge of having to fold myself into a modified apple box), being hauled through the orchards and around the pumpkin patch behind a big, green John Deere. On my debut run, Farmer Bob is at the wheel.

Farmer Bob is as real as it gets. He's passionate about agriculture and its history in the area. On his tour I learn a lot about Lord Aberdeen, the early planting of fruit trees in the Okanagan and how irrigation made orchards viable on dry hillsides. And I'm learning this history from a guy who's part of it. Farmer Bob represents the second generation to work the twenty-four hectare Davison farm (and two more are following him).

Auntie May and Uncle Tom got things started in 1933 and Bob joined the operation full time when his uncle passed away. The founders are remembered in the converted 1948 farmhouse called Auntie May's—a gift shop when I first saw it, but things are always evolving at Davison's and it's morphed into Auntie May's Deep Dish Cafe.

At a Glance

Davison Orchards is located at 3111 Davison Road, Vernon. Open daily from May 1 to October 31. Along with seasonal produce, farm-made preserves and country giftware, Davison offers a variety of kid-friendly activities (see chapter 10), weekend special events, snacks at the Picker Snack Shack and lunch at Auntie May's Deep Dish Cafe. Visit www.davisonorchards.ca for details or call 250.549.3266.

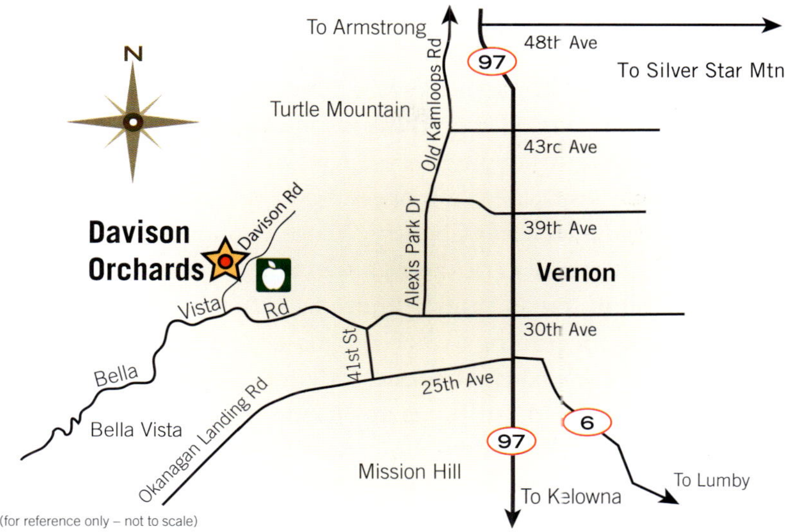

This is a country kitchen kind of place where you order from the counter and carry your food to tables in the little dining room or outside to the patio next to the kiddie's playground. Both provide nice valley views. The menu is simple—homemade soup, farm produce, fresh baked bread and fresh pressed apple juice—but there's no shortage of creativity with the ingredients. My hands-down favourite is the Harvest sandwich—sweet red peppers, ham, light cream cheese, cranberry jalapeño jelly and sliced apple grilled on whole wheat. I ask you—who thought to put sliced apple on a ham sandwich? Sheer genius.

But while I enjoy the sandwiches, Davison's signature dish—the one that always knocks my socks off—the one I never miss—the one I drive half the length of the valley for—is the almost-like-my-grandma-baked pie. Available at Auntie May's and the Apple Crate Bakery, the recipes are developed right on the farm and they add a new creation to the line-up every year. I could stand there all day just inhaling the cinnamon and butter emanating from apple pies that I know from experience taste subtly different as the season progresses and new varieties ripen. And what can I say about the hand rolled crust so light and flaky and rich (sorry, but we're on my favourite theme here) … and the apple crate berry filling (raspberry, blueberry, blackberry, apple and rhubarb)—sigh.

"Five minutes to peach pie," the baker calls from the back room.

Be still my beating heart. The women working the counter (kitted up in white aprons with cute little logos) look relieved. Late on a Sunday afternoon, stock on the shelves is noticeably thin. I'm not the only customer eager to carry off everything the kitchen can turn out, which keeps the peeling crew hopping.

Since my early visits, the whole operation has expanded exponentially into the Davison Orchards Country Village. Along with all the goodies in the Apple Crate Bakery, there's a selection of preserves like jams and apple butter in Nana's Pantry. Tamra tells me that Dora Davison—that's Bob's wife (beginning to feel like you need a program?)—once did the preserves one batch at a time. Judging by the volume of sales, I'd be surprised if she can still keep up on her own, but I can vouch for the fact that the apple butter still tastes homemade.

Whatever produce is in season is laid out for sale in the big red barn, but the specialty is definitely apples. The Davison's grow a wide range starting with tart summer varieties like Transparents and Sunrise, that are picked in late July and August, then swing into the fall harvest of McIntosh, Royal Galas, Arlets and on and on—the later season apples have a crisper texture, higher sugar content and longer shelf life.

Apples highlight their own festival every September. But Eve's fruit isn't the only attraction. From blossom time in spring through to the Family Pumpkin Festival in October (read more on this in chapter 10), Davison's is a fun place to reconnect with my agricultural roots—or just head for the bakery.

Davison Orchards, Vernon.

Pumpkin hoedown at the annual pumpkin fest.

Apple samples in the farm market.

Kelowna Land & Orchard Company

IF THE TERM "APPLE TATTOO" puts you in mind of dainty dermal decoration or beefy biker body art, you need to take the tour at this Kelowna farm. Every day, from spring through autumn, Rick Schmidt mounts the bright yellow tractor that draws two hayride wagons, and launches into his orchard oration—including the secret of how to tattoo Fuji apples.

For most of the forty-five minute tour, Rick twists in his seat to face the crowd filling the wagons. He grips the microphone with one hand and punctuates his narrative with the other. (Self-steering tractor?) Occasionally he casts an over-the-shoulder glance to confirm that we're still centred between the trees. The only time he interrupts his commentary is when he has to take the wheel to round the end of a row.

Rick has worked at Kelowna Land & Orchard Company for years, turning his hand to whatever needs doing—planting, pruning, thinning. His knowledge, experience and obvious attachment to the business come through loud and clear in the exuberant presentation.

Established in 1904, KLO is in its third generation of ownership by the Bullock family. John and his wife Bertha bought the property in 1942 and continue to live at the orchard in a farmhouse built in the 1920s. But they've passed the torch to their son Richard, his wife Jacqui and their children Nicole and John.

Today, the orchard covers over fifty-six hectares with two hundred thousand trees producing a whopping four million pounds of fruit annually. While pears, cherries, peaches, plums and apricots figure in the mix, apples make up by far the largest proportion.

On tour, Rick explains that different varieties, such as golden delicious, McIntosh and Spartans, are planted in three-row groups to facili-

At a Glance

Kelowna Land & Orchard Company is located at 2930 Dunster Road about ten minutes from downtown Kelowna. The orchard tour wagon rides and petting zoo make this a family fun destination, while the Farm Store and Raven Ridge Cidery broaden the appeal. The Ridge restaurant is open for lunch from May to October. For general information visit www.k-l-o.com.

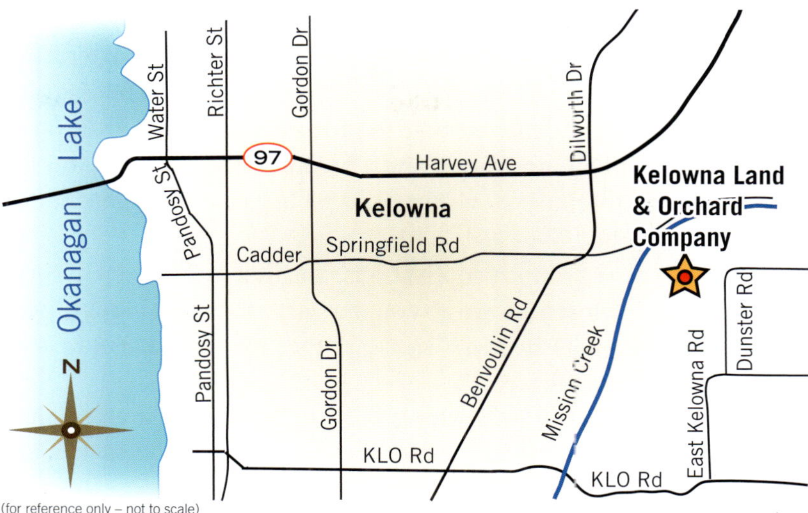

(for reference only – not to scale)

tate cross-pollination. In spring the orchard literally hums as bees work their magic, making some wonderful blossom honey in the process.

Rumbling along we see how the familiar silhouette of graceful trees, with tall triangular ladders propped among their branches, is giving way to modern dwarf plantings. Orchards of the future actually look more like vineyards. High-yield trees are set at four-foot intervals with their branches trained to follow supporting stringers. Several narrow rows can fit in the space occupied by one line of round, spreading trees. They're easy to irrigate and, being low to the ground, easy to pick. Remarkably, as many as two hundred prime apples will grow on a single tree.

Rick also proudly describes many of the environmentally friendly methods KLO uses. For example, rather than burning the mountains of suckers pruned from the trees each winter and adding to air pollution (not a pretty picture in the valley every spring), they're chipped and spread on the soil. Toxic sprays are kept to a minimum and pests like the codling moth are meeting their nemesis through Sterile Insect Release (SIR). Rick really warms to his subject as he describes all the ways they've found to trick these pesky critters. But he's very careful not to disturb the woodchucks peeking from under a stack of packing boxes and he beams as he tells of sighting deer in the orchard.

When the tour wraps up, a hostess appears with a tray load of KLO apple juice for us to sample. Often Richard Bullock, the mastermind behind the agri-tourism business, is also around to say hello. Back in the 1990s Richard realized that the future viability of fruit farming would depend on innovation and a broader perspective. It was his idea to open the orchard to visitors and he began to welcome educational tours in 1995.

Richard had two primary motivations. The first was to keep his own kids interested. "Most kids are leaving the farm today, not looking forward to working on it," he says. "Heck, it's the only way I know to keep the kids at home on the farm."

The second was more far reaching. "City kids don't know where their food comes from other than the grocery store. It's a good way to show them that apples grow on trees and not in baskets."

With the tours came the Farm Store, a country market selling farm-picked fruit in season, local crafts and preserves. And the enterprise just kept expanding. When you hop off the hay wagon, there's always a farm dog or two with a tail-wagging greeting. And I'm the biggest kid of all when it comes to the petting zoo where some of the sheep, rabbits and sky-dwelling goats, now living a life of leisure, are refugees from less happy circumstances.

Richard is a master at turning situations around. A few years ago, when an early frost caught the fruit still on the trees, instead of trashing the crop, he turned the frostbitten apples over to veteran winemaker Richard Wong. Next thing you knew, Raven Ridge Cidery was born and the orchard had yet another attraction.

KLO's Farm Store is definitely the only fruit stand in the Okanagan with a tasting room that serves up samples of apple ambrosia, a dry sparkling cider made with Braeburn apples, and a variety of iced apple ciders that are absolute joy for this Icewine lover.

Rounding out the orchard attractions is The Ridge restaurant, serving lunches with a side of lake and city views. The menu features local and natural ingredients in a relaxed country setting from mid-April through October.

But for me, KLO is still all about the apples. And if you want to know how they get those tattoos, you'll have to hop on a wagon and ask Rick.

Pioneer Country Market

"SPUDNUTS!" CRIES BRUCE. "We've got spudnuts in Kelowna."

"We do? That's great…. What's a spudnut?"

My man's story of sneaking into the bakery in his hometown of Sarnia, Ontario, to buy treats when he and his buddies were supposed to be heading to a neighbouring school for shop class, makes it clear that spudnuts meant much more to him than the mere pleasure of deep fried potato flour donuts. Clearly I can never develop a similar emotional attachment, but I'm still keen to give them a try.

We set out on a Saturday morning, pedaling our bikes south on Benvoulin Road to Pioneer Country Market. Saturday is the day that Velma Sperling rises even earlier than usual to begin the lengthy process of turning yeast, wheat and potato flour into happiness. It takes most of the morning to do her magic as she waits for the dough to rise and punches it down three times. Since Velma makes only one batch, timing is critical. Arrive at the market too early and the spudnuts aren't ready. Get there much past eleven and they're all gone.

We roll in about fifteen minutes past zero hour and take our place in line. Velma doesn't impose strict quotas, but there seems to be an unspoken sense of fair play among the faithful—or maybe it's something more basic. It occurs to me that anybody foolhardy enough to try to buy up more than their share would be unlikely to make it out the door alive. In truth, though, there's more of a sense of camaraderie among the Saturday morning faithful. As newcomers we're even welcomed.

We order a half-dozen and a couple of coffees. Grease spots are already seeping through the brown paper bag as we settle at a sunny table in the yard. Next to us, a young mom doles out treats to a trio of bouncing boys. At another table, four seniors are digging into their ration. Bruce dips his hand into our bag and presents me with

At a Glance

Look for the Pioneer Country Market at 1405 Pioneer Road on the east side of Benvoulin Road, just north of the Father Pandosy Mission in Kelowna. Open daily from April through late fall. Phone 250.762.2544.

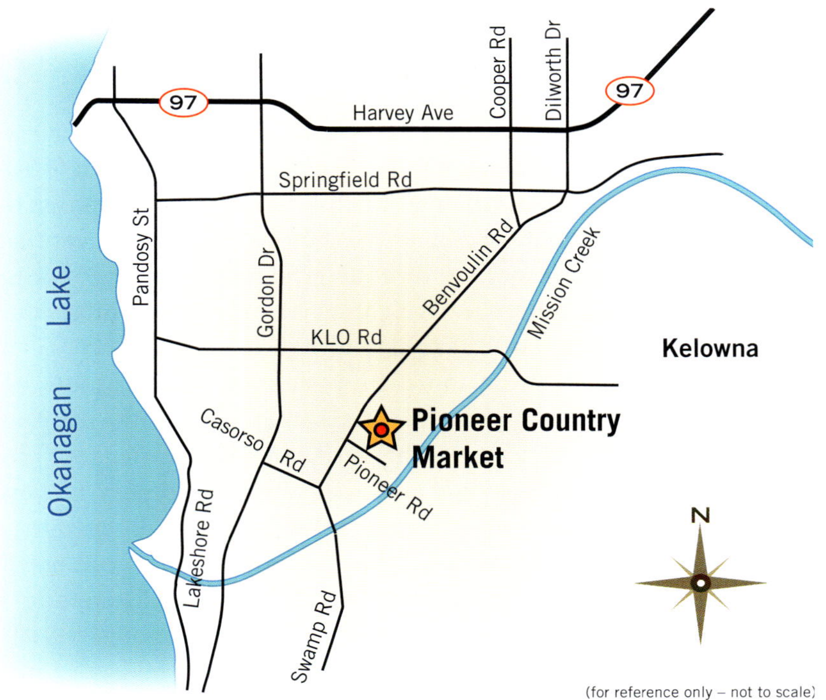

(for reference only – not to scale)

my very first spudnut. It looks like an ordinary donut with the traditional hole-in-the-middle shape, fried until the outside is golden and slightly crisp. I bite.

What can I say—creamy-white centre, soft and chewy, the comforting, luscious, heavenly taste of fat and flour. *Don't talk to me about cholesterol.*

Bruce is a dunker, so his standard is a donut that can stand up to immersion. I think he's nuts. Who, I ask, would want to dampen that perfect crispness? Why confuse enraptured taste buds. I say, let the spudnuts stand on their own. Clearly I've become an instant addict. I should be embarrassed to admit that we power through the entire bag, right there. Three spudnuts each (well, it would have been criminal to let them go stale).

In our defense, I point out that spudnuts aren't the only reason we like the market. Sometimes we drop by on a weekday, when temptation is out of reach and it's easier to focus on the other baked goods, like homemade pie. The rhubarb is inspirational—just the right blend of sweet-tartness to zing your taste buds without too much mouth-pucker—and a crust so flaky I'd rank it close to my mom's.

And preserves, all the traditional favourites from peach jam and mincemeat to pickled beans and sunshine relish. With a modern twist on an old theme, there's jalapeno jelly (both hot and sweet) and what Velma declares is the valley's first Okanagan Wine Jelly.

Some of the recipes are new; others go back to the earliest settlement of the region. The Pioneer Country Market comes by its name honestly. It sits on land bought in 1876 by John Casorso, one of the first five Italian families to settle here. Together with his eight sons and one daughter, he farmed the property surrounding Father Pandosy's Mission. They grew mixed crops of potatoes, corn, tobacco and onions—especially onions. John Casorso was the Onion King. The market now occupies the site of his record-breaking 1909 crop.

Over the next generations, the Casorso's diversified into a broader range of farming and ranching, but their reputation for quality produce never diminished. They always sold fruit and vegetables from

Saturday morning is the only time to get spudnuts at Pioneer Country Market.

their doorstep. In 1985, John's granddaughter, Velma, carried on the tradition and, with her daughter Karen, opened what has become a Kelowna landmark.

Just minutes from downtown, this is a hybrid country experience. True to the family tradition, they still sell their own fresh Okanagan produce. And along with the pies and breads and preserves they offer a popular selection of take-home-and-bake lasagna, meat pies, soups, perogies and noodles.

Back to that first spudnut quest. When the bag is empty we explore further. Despite the recent pigout, the scent of warm cinnamon buns nearly kills me as we browse among the crafts made by Okanagan artists and it follows us up the stairs to the museum loft. We find historic photos of lake steamers and the Mission Creek School (1908 to 1948), and I'm especially interested in a newspaper account of Kelowna's Chinatown, which I've never heard of to this point. The trove of artifacts includes antique hobbyhorses and a treadle Singer sewing machine (identical to the one in my grandma's dining room on which I made my first dress).

Since then we've been back lots of times for lunch. The soup is homemade, sandwich bread is fresh from the oven and the Caesar dressing is a classic. The atmosphere inside is cute-country, but on a hot summer day, the veranda's the place to be. Overlooking the maple-shaded lawn that replaced John Casorso's onion patch (and site of our first spudnut binge), it's a wide cool space screened with leafy vines. Long, sticky flypapers hanging from the rafters remind me of my grandma's farm kitchen or summers at my girlfriend's cottage. And when a John Deere rumbles past, looking purposeful and dragging a hay rake, I know I'm on a working farm.

If you drop by the market on a Saturday morning, we may meet. I'll be one of the folks wearing the rapturous grin of a spudnut addict with a fresh fix.

Kelowna
Farmers' and Crafters' Market

MY MAN AND I ARE MARKET JUNKIES. We love the colour and the smells and actually getting to know the people who produce our food. So we hit the Kelowna market pretty regularly. We'd go more often, but this place can be dangerous. I'm warning you, do not eat breakfast before approaching this market. Any attempt to deny the urge to stuff your mouth while stuffing your shopping bag will invariably prove injurious to your health—both physical and mental. I defy anyone to make it more than half way down the first aisle (any aisle) without eliciting a salivary reaction.

At the market, noshing and browsing go hand in glove, like sushi and soy sauce or pretzels and mustard or fruity crepes and—anything. And what are you going to do when a vendor calls out, "Try a tree-ripe…" and thrusts a luscious purple plum into your hand. It would be rude to refuse.

You might as well just get with the program and prepare to indulge your midline bulge while you check out the goodies and the characters hawking them. The place is like a self-serve circus. Show me the big box grocery emporium where you'll find a guy in a twenty-five gallon Stetson suggesting recipes for his blue potatoes or a lady tidying rows of bottles saying, "This is the hot zone, it's safe from the Peach Chipotle on."

Who needs a mall when you can walk around in the sunshine collecting up the ingredients for dinner—lamb chops and the rub to spice them; salad greens (and reds and yellows) and the vinaigrette

At a Glance

The Kelowna Farmers' and Crafters' Market is held at the corner of Dilworth and Springfield roads every Wednesday and Saturday, 8 a.m. to 1 p.m., from the beginning of April through the end of October. A Thursday evening market sets up in the Dolphins parking lot at the corner of Water Street and Sunset Drive, 4 p.m. to 8 p.m., from early June through Labour Day. Visit www.kelownafarmersandcraftersmarket.com for details.

to dress them; seedlings to grow the herbs to make your own seasonings; wood and pottery vessels to serve in; wine racks from which to select your favourite vintage; honey to sweeten dessert; an apron to keep your clothes clean; soap to wash up when you're done; and slippers to warm your tootsies when you collapse into an easy chair after the feast—if you have room for another meal after your grazing (oops) shopping expedition.

Don't say I didn't warn you.

Getting to know the people who grow our food at Kelowna Farmers' and Crafters' Market.

Carmelis Goat Cheese Artisan

THIS ULTRA-MODERN FARMGATE OPERATION south of Kelowna near Okanagan Mountain Park clings to the steep terrain beloved of the critters that give the milk that makes the cheese. Carmelis is the haven of Ofer and Ofri Barmor, who came to Canada from Israel to establish a safer life for their two daughters. But their dream took a terrifying detour in August 2003, four days after they moved the goats into the barn, when the Okanagan Mountain Park Fire forced them to flee.

Ofri and I are leaning on the half door of the barn, looking in on the goats as she recalls the day when people they'd never met turned up to help. "In Israel," she says, "there's no evacuation notice—just suicide bomb and done." Here, half-an-hour after an appeal went out over a local radio station, ten pickups with trailers had pulled into their lane. Neighbours found an alpaca farmer in East Kelowna who could make room for the ninety goats. Later in the long fire ordeal, the Barmor's were evacuated again. This time the goats found refuge at the Old Mac-Donald's Farm attraction (since leveled for commercial development.) "I'm proud to be part of a community that helps like this," says Ofri.

In all the family was out of their new home for a month. The wildfire reduced their nearly complete goat cheese operation to ashes and badly damaged the house. But in early October they began to clear the site and rebuild and by February, Ofer had made their first cheese.

Ofri gives me a special tour of the spotless dairy and then we descend into the cool, deliciously cheesy-smelling aging cellar, a cave built into the rock where the climate control doesn't have to do much work. We walk among huge rounds of goat Gruyer and big open racks, some holding cut and packaged cheeses like Vintage, a cheese that's

At a Glance

Carmelis is ideally situated for tasters on the south Kelowna wine trail at 170 Timberline Drive, twelve kilometres from the city centre near the entrance to Okanagan Mountain Provincial Park. The cheese (and gelato) shop is open from March 1 to mid-October. Details and online shopping at www.carmelisgoatcheese.com.

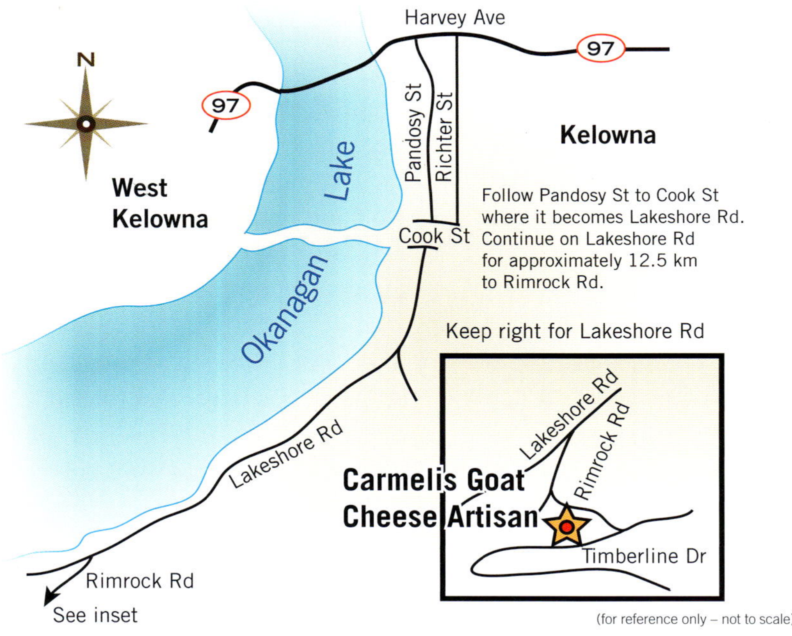

soaked for five days in Cedar Creek Pinot Noir then aged about two years, and Lior (named for one daughter), made with peppercorns and wrapped in bay leaves.

Hard cheeses like Goat Gonzola, which ages in pierced bags to let in the oxygen needed to grow veins of mould, and Carmel (named for the other daughter) are made from raw milk, while the soft cheeses like ash coated Misty (it's a French thing, nothing to do with the fire), Camembert-style Big White, and creamy, mushroom-toned Moonlight, use pasteurized.

When Ofri starts pointing out the fresh cheeses—Chevry (plain and herbed), feta and yogurt cheese—I wonder aloud just how many varieties they make. "Twenty to twenty-three," she says, "depends on the mood of my husband." Over the course of sixteen years the couple travelled throughout Europe "picking up ideas here and there." Ofer likes to try new things like the PecoBlue, which didn't work as a chevre but turned into something else. Ofri says, "When it's gone, it's gone."

And the creativity in this team doesn't stop with Ofer's cheese-making skills. Ofri has taken it into her head to add gelato to the product mix—bringing bliss to scores of overheated summer tourists (and me). The vibrant colours and swirling textures of the gelato cooler are like a work of abstract art in the crowded tasting room and don't get me started on the taste. Twenty-four luscious flavours imported from Italy (okay, I can't help it)—rich dark chocolate, crème brule, tiramisu, pistachio and how about that drunken plum, made with Ofri's homemade jam—whipped into homemade gelato onsite. Seriously!

I'm so glad the Barmor's decided to settle here.

Cheese tasting at Carmelis
Goat Cheese Artisan.

Sassy goat.

Lake Breeze, Naramata Bench. Facing page: Burrowing Owl vineyards, Black Sage Road, Oliver.

Chapter 7

Wine Time

WHAT I KNOW ABOUT WINE fits pretty easily into this chapter, so understand that you're definitely getting the Everyman perspective here. As a journalist and travel writer working in the Okanagan, I've learned a certain amount by osmosis, soaking up bits of knowledge (along with a considerable amount of premium vino priced far beyond my budget) at various press functions. I also had the good sense to marry a guy who's sipped through the major wine regions of the world on the trail of stories for Toronto-based magazines. To him I owe a debt for patient, personal tutelage. Yet in spite of all these resources, I remain an oenological babe-in-the-woods. The fact is, I just don't care enough about the details to study properly and make the knowledge stick. I'm way too happy popping around the valley, dropping into wineries, sipping the latest and leaving the buying decisions to Bruce. I admit I've barely made it past the red-with-meat, white-with-fish stage. He lives in hope that I will one day manage a credible wine and food pairing on my own and who am I to dash his hopes. Take it for what it's worth, here are my thoughts on wine touring in the Okanagan.

GPS Guide

I CAN'T KEEP UP. When I recently pulled out a wine country map, I found myself up to my barrel stopper in Black Widows and Black Clouds, Golden Beavers and Working Horses, Howling Bluffs and Volcanic Hills, Zero Balances and Ruby Tuesdays. It makes my head spin (and that's before I start tasting.) Imagine my joy when news of a high-tech helper pops into my inbox. Gypsy Guide, which offers in-car GPS guided audio tours for the Rockies and Calgary/Vancouver/Victoria corridor, has inserted a special Okanagan wine tour into the program.

It works like the familiar GPS mapping systems that help you find the next Tim's on the highway when your hubby won't stop and ask for directions, delivering verbal driving directions through the car's audio system. The location information, tour guide commentary and even onscreen photos are triggered as you reach particular geo co-ordinates—and they're pretty much spot on.

I collect my tour guide at the Kelowna Visitor Centre on Highway 97, install the suction cup holder on my windshield and mount the Blackberry-sized unit (plugged into the auxiliary radio socket), connect the power source and listen to the introductory audio—in less than ten minutes. A pretty significant accomplishment for somebody who prefers the I'd-rather-do-it-myself approach to sensibly following the step-by-step instructions illustrated on large laminated cards provided with the package.

For the next two days I allow myself to be guided around the region by a trio of disembodied voices. They soon begin to feel so much like real travel companions that names pop into my head. (Okay, so this doesn't happen until after the first tasting.)

Anyway, "Jack" strikes me as an all-business kind of guy who wants to

At a Glance

Gypsy Guide Tours are available online at www.gpstourscanada.com with pickup at Kelowna, Penticton or Osoyoos visitor centres. You can return the unit to the point of origin or, for an extra fee, to any Okanagan location, plus Vancouver, Victoria, Calgary, Edmonton or Jasper.

make sure I get the relevant overview for each town as I drive south from Kelowna. He suggests some good side trips—one to Skaha Bluffs and another to the Summerland Steam Train—that I obediently check out.

"Meg" has a habit of suddenly erupting from the speaker without notice, as if cued by an unseen tag-team signal they've got going inside the radio. She gives a lot of the left and right turn instructions and I come to rely on her excellent driving directions with lots of advance warning of lane changes and enough time for me to figure out whether I should flick on the left indicator—or the other left.

And when Jack is tired (or making a pit stop), she takes over the general commentary. It's Meg who tells me all about Mount Boucherie: a volcanic stump, the remainder of a mountain that peaked at more than 2,100 metres in elevation—sixty million years ago. Thanks, Meg.

My hand's down favourite, though, is definitely "Sue." Her bouncy delivery, reserved for the select wine-touring crowd, is always enthusiastic and often chuckle-inducing—like her explanation of where the name Dirty Laundry comes from (ask Sue, she'll tell you about the brothel—or find out for yourself later in this chapter). Anyway, I'm also proud to report that, while I did occasionally break into a grin, at no time did I actually speak to her (or Jack or Meg).

Summerhill Pyramid Winery, Kelowna.

Although this gismo is undeniably companionable, it is still just a machine and there are limitations on how much information can be delivered in this format. Certainly, guidebooks provide greater scope and depth. And no serious wine tourist should hit the road without reference to John Schreiner's *Okanagan Wine Tour Guide*, but it's a lot safer when you're driving to tune in a voice than to try flipping pages. Also, the freedom this tour provides goes a long way toward making up for the deficiencies.

While only seventeen of the valley's gazillion wineries are currently included (those that paid sponsorship fees) the tour routes put you right in the thick of tasting territory and you can stop, or not, anywhere you like. There's no set itinerary and lots of independent travellers will gladly forego the benefit of a living, breathing tour guide who can answer questions along the way, in exchange for complete freedom from group constraints and the tyranny of a schedule.

Something I really love about my electronic guides is that they uncomplainingly pick up wherever I leave off. When I decide to hang around the barrel room at Rollingdale, chatting it up with owner Steve Dale until he goes outside to fire a new bird-scaring pistol (which he lets me try—yee-haw!), Sue is ready as soon as I start to roll.

"Turn left at the next intersection," she says and continues with instructions to guide me through a crosshatch of side streets back to the highway.

It's the same on Naramata Road when I spot The Trail Store, a photogenic little fruit stand half hidden by an apple-laden orchard. A two-minute photo-break stretches into nearly an hour, getting to know Rod Hollett and hanging out on the patio under the plum trees with cyclists who stop for a snack as they ride the KVR Trail between Penticton and Naramata. Sue doesn't mind waiting. When I get back in the car, she just carries on with her description of the wineries of the Naramata Bench and says nothing when I decide not to stop. I've visited pretty much all of them, and besides, a sign for an art show snags my attention.

Down a side road and along a narrow lane, I find a surprising sculpture garden, studio and gallery on the grounds of a blindingly white Louisiana Georgian house, the Unique Bed and Breakfast. Another half hour slips away. By the time I get headed for the wineries of the Okanagan's deep south, it's well past noon and I have to zip along. Meanwhile, Sue is tireless with backstories like the naming of See Ya Later Ranch and the characteristics of the Golden Mile versus Black Sage Bench. And Jack and Meg chime in with such info bits as bird watching at Vaseux Lake and the founding of Oliver.

One drawback to the system is that you don't know in advance exactly which wineries are included (unless you're clever enough to check online). Had I known, I would have covered the eight stops from Kelowna to Summerland in one day and the remaining nine clustered in the South Okanagan on day two.

Still, I honestly feel a twinge at parting—and I never do figure out how to leave Sue, Meg and Jack a tip.

Quail's Gate
Okanagan Winery,
West Kelowna.

Crushing at Calona
Vineyards, Kelowna.

Bottling at Township 7,
Naramata Bench.

Laurie's Unofficial Wine Tour

THERE IS NO IGNORING the insistent thump in my chest. Though I sit perfectly still—and can't claim any greater exertion than walking through the portal that separates a brilliant Okanagan summer afternoon from the cool depths of a miniature replica of Egypt's pyramid of Cheops—my heart is racing. Remarkably, I find the sensation so pleasant that instead of leaping to the conclusion that I'm about to keel over from a massive coronary, I begin to seriously believe in the positive energy that the (some would call eccentric) owner of Summerhill Pyramid Winery is explaining.

I've caught a particular break today as Stephen Cipes takes the time to personally describe his reasons for constructing this geometrically precise building for aging barrels and finishing his award-winning wines. Stephen is passionate about all things natural. Like a growing number of Okanagan wineries, his vineyards are completely organic, though no one else has yet gone to the extreme of building a pyramid to apply the power of sacred geometry to their products.

My heart continues to pound as I quietly sit among the barrels, enveloped in their earthy smell, and let my eyes follow the straight lines of the building's wooden beams to the apex of four precise triangles far overhead. This is not the experience I expected when we began the day's wine touring with our current round of visitors.

Playing tour guide is a residential hazard here in the valley. Our

At a Glance

If you're not staying in our guestroom, professionally guided tours help eliminate the boggle factor and they're also a great idea if your spitting technique still needs work. With somebody else driving, you can swallow all the samples your liver can handle. Conventional itineraries include several wineries and lunch but there are plenty of more adventurous options pairing wine tours with everything from cycling and wildflower viewing to golf, skiing and floatplane flights. Four annual festivals—Spring, Summer, Fall and Icewine—celebrate the grape with hundreds of events and activities. Get details at www.owfs.com. Visitor centres in every Okanagan community stock wine touring maps and brochures, information on individual wineries and tour companies.

spare bedroom gets a pretty good workout from June through September. And who's complaining. Visitors give us a great excuse to keep up with the wine scene.

I'm thunderstruck by the industry's explosion in the two decades I've called the Okanagan home, from a few scattered vineyards to an internationally recognized appellation with at least one hundred and sixteen wineries as I write. Trying to keep up with the annual crop of new establishments and organizing outings to sample the complexity of the valley's many sub-regions is daunting. There is no possibility of covering more than a fraction. Bruce is infinitely more knowledgeable than I am, but at least I've learned to swirl-sniff-sip—and even spit—without embarrassing myself.

Kelowna

Around Kelowna alone, there are enough wineries to cram a couple of days of touring. We usually hit the tasting rooms on the west-

Howard Soon, Sandhill's master winemaker.

ern-facing slopes of the South Mission where the vineyards range down the mountainsides to the shores of Okanagan Lake, gaining maximum sun exposure and giving our guests the signature wine country views they expect.

Between swirl-sniff-and-sips (most of the guests can't bring themselves to spit) of Cedar Creek's Pinot Noir, St. Hubertus's Pinot Blanc and Summerhill's Cipes Brut champagne-style sparkling wine, we slip in a side trip to one of the valley's best agri-destinations, Carmelis Goat Cheese Artisan (see chapter 6). There we indulge in a sinful gelato, add the other half of a wine and cheese picnic to the collection of clinking bottles in the trunk and repair to the nearest beach for lunch and a dip.

Our tasting trail continues in south Kelowna at Tantalus Vineyards, noted for its Old Vines Riesling (produced from vines planted in 1978) and moves on to a fusion of old and new Okanagan agriculture at Raven Ridge Cidery. Located at Kelowna Land & Orchard Company (also appearing in chapter 6), the cidery produces five varieties of iced cider (like Icewine) from Anjou pears and Fuji, ambrosia, Braeburn and Granny Smith apples, and the truly unusual Truly Sparkling Cider.

Lake Country

Lake Country, north of Kelowna, is home to more wineries of note. Ex Nihilo, Intrigue and Arrowleaf Cellars are relative newcomers, but wines like Arrowleaf's Bacchus white blend are pulling in the awards. Nearby Gray Monk, on the other hand, is a perennial favourite, owned by the Heiss family who were among the industry's pioneers. We often time our tours to hit Gray Monk's Grapevine Restaurant around the lunch hour and settle under an umbrella on the patio to regard (with a tasting-induced glaze) the vineyards, lake and far-shore ridges—while adding to the buzz with a three wine sample flight. My selection always includes their Pinot Auxerrois and something from the Latitude 50 series.

Quail's Gate vineyard on the slopes of Mount Boucherie, West Kelowna.

Gray Monk Estate Winery, Lake Country.

Not Icewine on the vine. These grapesicles were created when irrigation water froze.

Mount Boucherie

On the west side of Okanagan Lake another group of wineries clusters on and around the flanks of Mount Boucherie. Not far from downtown Kelowna across the lake via the William R. Bennett floating bridge, they provide a new perspective on the scenery and a number of wines that showcase the unique characteristics of Mount Boucherie's volcanic soil.

The experience on this side of the lake is eclectic with everything from a casual tasting bar set up in a Quonset hut at Rollingdale and the garage-like building at Beaumont through the middle of the road Mt. Boucherie wineshop to the sunset view from the patio of Old Vines Restaurant at Quail's Gate. Mission Hill is probably the most visually stunning winery in the valley with its mission-inspired (what else?) architecture, stupendous vistas and twelve-storey bell tower (complete with carillon) high on a shoulder of Mount Boucherie. Be prepared to dodge the wedding parties on Saturdays.

I think of these wineries as neighbours. We hear the carillon pealing out the noon hour as we pop the cork on a bottle of something local and prepare to linger over lunch in our garden and we keep a standing reservation for anniversary dinners at Old Vines.

Summerland's Bottleneck Drive

From here, sampling the rest of Okanagan wine country requires longer forays, even overnighters to the South Okanagan. Summerland makes a good daytrip. This little Tudor themed town offers some really good dining options and a seriously fun side trip on the Kettle Valley Steam Railway (more in chapter nine) along with eleven wineries (and counting) on its Bottleneck Drive route.

The McWatters family started Sumac Ridge Winery here over twenty-five years ago and their Cellar Door Bistro is one of those good dining spots. Another Summerland winery is proving that there is something in a name. Formerly called Scherzinger Vineyards, the rechristened Dirty Laundry label is gaining lots of consumer attention.

In his must-have *Okanagan Wine Tour Guide*, now in its third edition, wine guru John Schreiner says the second owner, Ron Watkins, borrowed from a Summerland story about an early 20th century Chinese railway worker who opened a laundry—with a brothel in the back room—which came to be known as the "dirty laundry."

Penticton VQA

Penticton is the gateway to the largest concentration of wineries and vineyards. When we have guests in tow, we usually start at the Visitor Centre VQA shop (VQA stands for Vintner's Quality Alliance, an Appellation of Origin system that stipulates quality standards and guarantees origin). Staff pour the day's spotlight wines and provide lessons in tasting technique. This is crucial for newbies who want to overcome the wine-mystique intimidation factor. My first experience here set me up for a lifetime of fearless tasting in even the most sophisticated circles. I may not know volumes about wine, but now I know how to look like I do.

"Let's face it," said Jolene, the sommelier on duty that day, "wine is a beverage made out of rotten grapes." *Good attitude. I can work with this.*

She took our little group through the full hands-on, nose-in-glass tasting demo that now allows me to swirl, sniff and sip with confidence. And I learned that if you really want to look like a cork dork (a good thing) or simply avoid an impaired driving charge after a day of tasting, you've got to learn to spit. Sure it's tough to get over the horror of publicly spewing a mouthful of $30-a-bottle Merlot into a spittoon, and tougher still to accomplish this feat without dribbling down your chin (aiming at the centre of the far wall of the receptacle and really shooting the wine out of my mouth works for me), but Jolene was adamant that spitters get respect. According to her, showing your technique (and by implication—your savvy) will often entice the winemaker to pull something really special out from under the counter.

At the very least you'll feel good about yourself. Last summer, after my aunt and cousin took the ten-minute course, they immediately tried their new skills at the next winery they visited. The two of them are still beaming about the tasting-room attendant who told them, "You two spit like pros."

Summerland Sweets is making fruit wines under the Sleeping Giant label.

Swirl, sniff, sip and spit — Wine Tasting 101 at the VQA shop in Penticton's Visitor Centre.

Naramata Bench

Northeast of Penticton, it's easy to spend a weekend on the wineries of the Naramata Bench (thirty of them at last count), which craft the full range of Okanagan wines with notable Merlot, Syrah and Cab Merlot blends. This area has to be the biggest surprise for people who vacationed here as kids and haven't been back for awhile. The orchards that once covered the slopes and transformed the hillsides into a fragrant garden with each year's blossom season are disappearing as fast as you can say chop-down-the-trees-and-plant-vines.

One exception is Elephant Island where Miranda and Del Halladay have married orchard and winery to make fruit wines. Don't think cloying sweetness here, their black currant and crabapple varieties leave a nice tart pucker. They make a range of food-friendly fruit wines (yes, I'm talking fruit wine with steak), dessert wines and Stellaport.

Therapy Vineyards—really working a theme with inkblot labels and wines named Freudian Sip, Pink Freud and SuperEgo—is one of the newcomers, occupying the property where Red Rooster (now relocated and vastly expanded) got its start. These days, Red Rooster is making a memorable Reserve Merlot and showcases the work of local artists with an outdoor sculpture garden and indoor galleries. This is the home of the controversial sculpture *Frank the Baggage Handler* whose nudity sparked such a row in Penticton that he was removed from public display. Just as well, I'm sure he figures a winery garden is a big step up from a traffic circle.

Hillside, with its seventy-two foot tower and solid stone cellars dug into the hillside, has stayed put. I first learned about how rosé is made in Hillside's wine shop and tried a larger sample with lunch in the Barrel Room Bistro. Another popular summer lunch spot is the Mediterranean themed patio at Lake Breeze. Wine and cheese come together in the tasting room at Poplar Grove where you can sample the winery's vintages along with the creamy Camembert and blue cheeses they craft onsite. Foodie alert—this cheese is awesome.

In the village of Naramata, which I think truly deserves its certification by the international Cittaslow movement (think Slow Food on a community scale), our go-to spot is Cobblestone in the Naramata Heritage Inn. Its cellar boasts some two hundred and twenty labels.

Frank the Baggage Handler in his new home at Red Rooster Winery on the Naramata Bench.

Sunset at Red Rooster Winery on the Naramata Bench.

One of the many works of art displayed in the sculpture garden and galleries at Red Rooster.

Okanagan Falls/Skaha Lake Corkscrew Drive

South of Penticton, a boggling number of wineries cluster in three areas. The Corkscrew Drive route around Okanagan Falls includes Blasted Church (great story involving dynamite), the highest elevation vineyards in the Okanagan (Hawthorne Mountain) and more of those catchy new names. Legend has it that in the 1920s, when Hawthorn Mountain owner Major Hugh Fraser's British wife decided she'd had enough colonial living and packed her bags, she left a note saying, "See ya later."

The winery adopted the phrase to brand its premium line, See Ya Later Ranch, which includes a wine called Ping, named for one of the major's beloved dogs—presumably kept to provide company after his wife decamped. Ping's headstone, along with one for each of the major's other canine companions, rests in a memorial enclave under a tree in front of the 1902 heritage house, now expanded with a tasting room, patio and the requisite stellar view.

Deploying bird nets at See Ya Later Ranch on the Corkscrew Drive wine route near Okanagan Falls.

Black Sage Road

Two more wine routes run south between Oliver and Osoyoos. The only winery actually located within the town of Oliver (self-styled the Wine Capital of Canada) is also the first winery on Black Sage Road on the east side of the valley. When Bruce, who acquired a soft spot for all things Portuguese while living in Toronto's Little Portugal and travelling in the country itself, discovered Quinta Ferreira, he instantly connected with the family-run operation and their wines. We never return from a trip to the South Okanagan without a stock of their German blend Mistura Branca, Quinta Ferreira Rosé and—for special dinners—their Obra-Prima.

Also among the fourteen wineries on Black Sage Road are Silver Sage, Oliver Twist and Black Hills (noteworthy for its Nota Bene blend and celebrity connection with part-owner Jason Priestly of *90210* fame) and the renowned Burrowing Owl. Here you can take a self-guided tour of the bell tower, interpretive displays, cellars and viewing platform, then dine in the Sonora Room restaurant and, if you've had the presence of mind to think far, far ahead and book a room, skip the whole designated driver thing and stumble from your table to a comfy bed in the luxury guest house.

Golden Mile

Across the valley the lucky thirteen line-up of Golden Mile wineries includes the likes of Fairview Cellars, Inniskillin, Gehringer Brothers, Road 13 and Tinhorn Creek where you can taste why you shouldn't turn up your nose at screw caps (a.k.a. Stelvins). Many wineries have started using them on their premium lines as the best way to avoid cork taint. Tinhorn Creek offers a self-guided winery tour, demonstration vineyard, art shows and a summer concert series in its outdoor amphitheatre. This is also one starting point for the Golden Mile hiking trail that nearly killed me (chapter 1)—with two- and ten-kilometre versions that take in ruins related to the Tinhorn Creek gold mine.

The demonstration vineyard and winery at Tinhorn Creek Vineyards on the Golden Mile south of Oliver.

John Ferriera dedicates a bottle to me at Quinta Ferriera Estate Winery on Black Sage Road, Oliver.

Osoyoos Lake Bench

At the southern end of the valley, the Osoyoos Lake Bench is gaining a foothold with several wineries including Lastella, Twisted Tree and North America's first aboriginal owned and operated winery, Nk'Mip Cellars. Apart from the fact that I'm partial to Nk'Mip Chardonnay and its peppery Merlot, this is a never-miss stop on our visitor tours. We don't usually take time for the winery tour, although it's a good one, but always plan on at least a couple of hours for the ecological and cultural experience of the Nk'Mip Desert Cultural Centre (chapters 5 and 8).

Lunch selections from the aboriginal-inspired menu on the winery's patio restaurant include salmon, bison and venison with a side of vineyard, desert and Osoyoos Lake views. For dinner, we like Passa Tempo, the intimate restaurant at the adjacent Spirit Ridge Resort and Spa (and site of the memorable dinner at which John Schreiner sat next to me and graciously sidestepped my comparative ignorance).

Downtown Kelowna

Occasionally our visitors are pressed for time and can't sip from winery to winery. We take them to Kelowna's downtown Cultural District where we drop by the tasting room at Calona Vineyards, BC's oldest continually operating winery (founded in 1932), where both Calona's Artist Series and winemaster Howard Soon's single vineyard Sandhill wines are available. Then we hit the historic Laurel Packinghouse, home of the BC Wine Museum and a VQA Wine Shop that hosts daily tastings and stocks a lot of vintages that you can't find anywhere else but the winery.

Nk'Mip Cellars in Osoyoos is North America's first aboriginal owned and operated winery.

Nk'Mip's wine boutique is part showroom, part aboriginal cultural experience.

Okanagan Summer Wine Festival

Tasting at the VQA shop is an efficient way to get a feel for the whole Okanagan wine scene, but it's nowhere near the most fun. I discovered the ultimate one-stop experience at the Okanagan Summer Wine Festival, held every year on the second weekend of August at Silver Star Mountain Resort.

Along with the obvious appeal of the venue, one of the things I love is the camaraderie that develops. At my first event (pairing chocolate and wine) I met a group of women who had flown in from Saskatchewan for their annual high-school-best-friends-getaway. At dinner that night—a rousing duel between Oliver Twist and Therapy Vineyards (what would Freud think) pitting one winery against the other over each of five courses—one of the school friends sat at the table I'd randomly selected and we soon also got to know the couple from Edmonton who shared with us.

Next day the whole crowd turned up for a guided hike from mountaintop to village in search of local lore, wildflowers and wild berries. We kept meeting like this through more chocolate and wine pairing, coffee and wine pairing, cheese and wine pairing (note my ever-present food theme). By the time we got to the signature progressive tasting—think giant block party featuring scores of Okanagan wines along with cheese and bread—we just expected to connect.

That's what I think wine touring should really be about. Meeting like-minded people, sampling outstanding vintages and good food, taking time to enjoy the Okanagan and savouring that nice little buzz.

Progressive tasting event at the
Okanagan Summer Wine Festival,
Silver Star Mountain Resort.

Think giant mountain
block party.

Culture Counts

IT'S EASY TO WRITE THE OKANAGAN off as a cultural backwater. Where, you might ask, do I see the latest Broadway musical, a professional production of King Lear, hear Ben Heppner sing Tristan und Isolde or catch Aleksandar Antonijevic dancing Onegin. Tell me where I can pop in to see an Emily Carr or take my kids and wow them with a Barosaurus skeleton. Not fair questions, I counter. You want metropolitan culture, you put up with the rest of metropolitan lifestyle. What you get in the valley is a rapidly developing regional cultural scene with some fun and quirky elements like theatre in a farmer's field. Our art galleries and museums continue to evolve and since UBC Okanagan set up shop, we've met eminent scholars, political figures and social activists on the lecture circuit. Many communities support dedicated amateur theatrical companies and the valley has long been a hotbed of musical talent. When I think culture in the Okanagan, I don't moan about what it's not, I marvel at what it is.

Kelowna Cultural District

"SHE'S 26 YEARS OLD," says a quiet voice to my left. Without changing position, my forearms crossed and resting on the wooden railing of a narrow bridge, I let my eyes follow the man's outstretched hand in the direction of an eighteen-inch black and white fish. She's swimming in lazy curves amid an orange and golden school of her fellow koi, their upturned mouths forming perfect Os in anticipation of the next ration of pellets he'll scatter. "Been here since the gardens opened," he continues.

I murmur, "Really," or something equally inane and continued to gaze at the circling fish. It's not that I'm brain dead or even terminally rude, it's just that Kasugai Gardens is such a tranquil place, so peace-inducing, that lengthy conversation seems out of place.

Originally created as a tribute to Kelowna's sister city, Kasugai, Japan, the little enclave remains a wonderfully calm retreat in the busy Cultural District. Sheltered behind thick walls with trickling waterfalls and fountains, the sound-muting greenery makes leafy bowers where you can eat lunch, read a book or just stare at infinity.

The matriarch swims out of sight beneath a green island of lily pads crowned by two perfectly formed pink blossoms.

A whole lot has changed in the streets beyond her pond since I first stood on that bridge two decades ago. The Cultural District—a six-block area bordered by historic Bernard Avenue, Kelowna's main downtown shopping street, and the waterfront district, with its pedestrian walkways, yacht club, green spaces and beaches—now hosts a bevy of museums and theatres, funky shops and eclectic galleries, chic bistros

At a Glance

Kelowna's Cultural District is a six-block area in the city's downtown core bordered by Clement Avenue, Ellis Street, Queensway and the lakeshore. It's chock-a-block with galleries, museums, performing arts venues, public art, boutiques, restaurants, parks and a VQA wine shop. To learn more about the District, visit www.artsinkelowna.com. Download a map and take the self-guided walking tour with seventeen stops highlighting art, history and nature. For more detailed info on public art in the Cultural District and around Kelowna, download the brochure, *Public Art*.

and ethnic eateries, waterfront resorts and trendy lofts. Back then it was a pretty mixed bag.

While a nucleus had formed—Kasugai Gardens, Kelowna Museums, Memorial Arena, Kelowna Art Gallery, Community Theatre and the newly renovated Laurel Packinghouse—they stood like lonely islands amid the seedy lots, run-down storefronts and light industrial lands that were once the heart of the region's fruit packing industry. The area wasn't much of a draw for locals or tourists.

But then, people weren't coming to Kelowna for culture. It was still a beach town with a little golf and skiing thrown in. Fruit production was still fairly big but agri-tourism was a new-age idea and Calona Wines was practically a solo act in the wine biz.

Then wineries started popping up like toadstools after a rain. Forget trying to keep track. At this moment the count has passed one hundred and sixteen in the Okanagan with over twenty in the Kelowna area alone. That growth has completely changed the character of tourism here. People still come for the outdoor stuff, but there's a whole new element looking for more "cultural pursuits."

Kelowna had actually started to develop a cultural vision as far back as the 1970s and in 2004, the city was named a Cultural Capital of Canada, which meant federal dollars. Long gone are the vacant lots and

Concept to Creation, sculpture outside Kelowna's Rotary Centre for the Arts.

paint-starved storefronts. The area is totally transformed.

Bruce and I are pretty frequent visitors. Before we take in a symphony performance at the Community Theatre or a concert at Prospera Place, we usually eat ethnic, Siam Orchid for Thai food or Bouchons Bistro for fabulous French.

Another good cultural haunt is the Okanagan Heritage Museum. This isn't a large facility, but it's laid out with the spatial trickery of Kasugai Gardens, and the limited area in this museum is expanded by a group of satellites. Next door, the Okanagan Military Museum occupies a nook in the Memorial Arena (Bruce loves this one). A block north on Ellis Street the BC Orchard Industry Museum and the BC Wine Museum share space in the Laurel Packinghouse. Dating to 1918, this is the oldest and largest standing packing house in British Columbia and Kelowna's first designated heritage building.

The Laurel also hosts a VQA (Vintner's Quality Alliance) wine store, which is handy if you don't have time to hit all those local wineries—or you're into one-stop shopping. Every day they pour a different flight for tasting and the shop stocks a good selection of BC vintages, some that you can't buy anywhere else but the winery. We never escape without a bag full of clinking bottles, so this is usually our last stop when we go walkabout—which is the only way to see the District.

We give our grandson Alex his first taste of the area one sunny Saturday morning when he's about a year-and-a-half old. He's perfectly satisfied to ride along in his stroller, babbling his impressions of the slanted wooden beams and curved roofline that make the Kelowna Public Library look like an open book with its two-storey window walls reflecting the colours of the art shop and dinner theatre on the opposite side of Ellis Street.

He reacts equally favourably to the galleries and antique shop in tiny Cannery Lane; doesn't have much to say about the display at the Kelowna Art Gallery, but really loves the whimsical masks that sculptor Iris Morden creates in her studio at the Rotary Centre for the Arts.

This multi-purpose facility is a cornerstone of the District. We've attended a variety of performances here including local singers doing Andrew Lloyd-Webber in the atrium and a touring ensemble that filled the intimate Mary Irwin Theatre with Mozart and Vivaldi.

The centre also houses a couple of commercial art galleries, free space that showcases local talent, a dance studio, pottery workshop and a series of individual studios where you can visit the resident artists as they paint, mould or chip away at works in progress.

"Come on in," says Iris as we tentatively wheel the stroller into the space she shares with fellow sculptor Mel Hunt. "We're just cleaning up from a show." That explains why Mel is wielding a paint roller instead of a hammer and chisel. They're both more than happy to drop everything and talk about their work. I think Mel would jump at any excuse to abandon that roller. And Iris patiently takes time to introduce Alex to her latest sculpture, encouraging him to run his little fingers over the smooth stone. He loves it.

But even the most artistic toddler reaches a saturation point and Alex is overjoyed when we release him on the grassy square of the Arts Common to join a mom and her two young boys kicking a soccer ball. While he lets off steam, we sit on a tree-shaded bench and toss around the idea of heading over to the waterfront and walking up to the Rotary Marshes along Brandt's Creek to check on the resident osprey family and duck population.

Alex settles the question as the soccer game winds down. He toddles over, grabs the handles of the stroller and starts pushing—in the opposite direction. Message received. We follow him along the Art Walk, a pathway covered by an expansive pergola supporting grape vines and bordered by mosaics of historic packing box labels and a progression of sculptures titled *Fruit Stand*. He stops in front of a halved peach and eyes it closely, his little head tilted to one side, a tiny frown creasing his brow. Not sure what that signifies—concentration, consternation, constipation.

He makes no comment and after a minute, returns to stroller pushing. At the end of the walkway we pass a cast bronze statue called *Sentinel* (since moved to the City Hall foyer), one of about a dozen works of public art concentrated in the District. Our budding art critic just motors on by. Right, then, enough art for one day. I suggest we carry on to Kasugai Gardens and stare at the fish. No argument.

Iris Morden in her studio at the Rotary Centre for the Arts, Kelowna.

The Maestra

A FEW YEARS AGO I attended a gala fundraiser for the Okanagan Symphony Orchestra (OSO). It included a concert and the standard cocktail intermission. The cocktails were okay, but I have to admit the music left me under-impressed. At the time I put it down to the unequal comparison of a regional orchestra with the major city symphonies I was used to hearing.

So why will you find Bruce and me at every OSO performance (despite no free wine or appies) ... because the OSO is a whole other deal these days, and I think it's because of the new presence on the podium—Maestra Rosemary Thomson (who everybody calls Rose).

We met over coffee at The Grand in the autumn of 2007. The symphony PR machine was trotting out its recently selected music director/ conductor to hype the upcoming season. I arrived early and asked for a centrally located table where I could watch the entrance—and what an entrance she made. Nothing pompous or flashy or overtly flamboyant, but the woman has presence—possibly aided by a wild mane of flaming red hair. Think Beethoven-Do—on steroids—in technicolour. You can't miss her.

The thirty minutes scheduled for our interview easily stretched into nearly two hours. It felt like I was talking to a girlfriend, except that along with the family anecdotes Rose managed to weave in a riveting music history lesson and such a sense of passion for her new role that I rushed back to the office and ordered season tickets. Talk about charisma—and then I saw her on stage.

Exhorting, coaxing, demanding … As I watched, no, as I sat riveted to her performance, the maestra physically drew the notes from the musicians, sedately marking time with her baton, sweeping her arms through lush melodies, stepping into emphatic phrases, rising on tip-

At a Glance

The Okanagan Symphony Orchestra performs in Kelowna, Vernon and Penticton. The season includes five main stage concerts plus a Christmas show and a post season special. Read all about it at www.okanagansymphony.com.

toe, her whole body vibrating as she drew them through a crescendo to the heroic climax of (wait for it) Beethoven's Eroica.

Rose makes no effort to contain her passion for the music or her enthusiasm for her move to the Okanagan. For a self-confessed "water girl" who grew up on the shores of Lake Ontario and loves hiking and biking, life in the Okanagan (after Calgary) looks pretty appealing. The wife and mother of two young children sees this as a family community.

A pianist, cellist and vocalist, Rose quips that she grew up in the "Family von Thomson." When mom, dad and seven kids piled into the station wagon (not equipped with a radio), they sang. Rose performed in her first Messiah when she was seven. Her road to the podium wasn't immediately obvious, but she does recall the moment it hit her. She was talking on a payphone at the University of Toronto, staring unfocused at a poster for a graduate conducting program. Aha!

When I ask the standard music-interview-for-dummies question about her favourite composer, she grins. "Yeah, it's a little bit like asking who your favourite child is, but I definitely have composers that really resonate with me—Beethoven," she says. "I mean, I love Mozart, I really do, but there's something about Beethoven. I think it's the organic rhythm—what he does with rhythm—that I find especially thrilling. I sense that more when I'm actually playing or conducting it than when I'm listening to it. I think that's because it's such physical music that to be engaged in the physical act of making that music it really, really touches something deep inside of you. I hope that translates to the listener, too."

Of course, there's more. "I love French music," she continues. "I love Debussy and Ravel, their use of colour in the orchestra. There's a sort of amorphousness. They've taken all the strong edges out. Not all the time, but I love that kind of quality, dreamy, all is right with the world."

And more … Rose loves opera and Bruce Springsteen and she's very open to contemporary sounds. I admire her commitment to showcasing modern Canadian composers, but I have to tell you, it often feels like I'm paying my dues as I sit through these segments in the first half of the program—just itching to get to (what my unsophisticated ear regards as) the good stuff. Rose says her programming will always reflect diversity because "the orchestra as pure entertainment is not something that I can buy into, because it's much bigger than that."

Her hope is to give audiences a "transforming experience." We may feel uplifted or angry or touched by our sadness, but she aims for the orchestra to provoke thought and feeling—to put us "in touch with the human experience, because that is what art is."

Rose prepares for concerts by immersing herself in the music and its historic context and this preparation comes through in her introductions to each composition. These mini master classes, like the one she delivered at our interview, are a trademark of her concerts and they add immeasurably to the experience for musical airheads like me.

Professionally, she says her goal is to make both the music and the orchestra accessible to the community through programs like her innovative pre-concert talks and *After Thoughts* where she plays talk-show host and chats up guest performers, members of the orchestra and anybody from the audience who wants to hang around after the show. To begin with *After Thoughts* was staged in the foyer, but it proved so popular that it soon moved into the auditorium to accommodate the numbers. This is just one of the pet outreach programs the maestra mentioned when we talked.

She's also masterminded a series of programs cleverly designed to put butts in seats. Along with favourites by Beethoven and Mendelssohn, Haydn, Straus, Schubert, Tchaikovsky, Mozart, Vivaldi and on and on—she's produced programs with stories to appeal to families; invited local amateur musicians like the Candesca Singers and the Kelowna Night Orchestra to perform with the symphony; brought in children's choirs and local soloists like the mind-boggling Alicia and Colleen Venables; and arranged guest performances by stars like David Greenberg. We've had opera and a massed choir that gave me goose bumps with Beethoven's *Ode to Joy*.

I don't know what she's done to fire up these musicians, clearly they were already a talented group, but the difference from my first encounter with the Okanagan Symphony is stunning and judging from the packed houses, the maestra's strategy for connecting the orchestra with Okanagan communities is working.

Nk'Mip Desert Cultural Centre

PRECIOUS LANDS, RARE CREATURES and ancient peoples—the Osoyoos Indian Band protects and provides insight into these treasures at the Nk'Mip (pronounced in-ka-meep) Desert Cultural Centre in Osoyoos. I've watched the centre evolve from a few exhibits in a portable prefab that I first saw in 2003 to one of the premier First Nations attractions in British Columbia. The cultural experience has always been top drawer.

A band member named Shelley gathers a small group on the deck of the prefab for a panoramic view of the twenty-hectare site and the surrounding four hundred and eighty-five hectares of desert, one of the largest continuous areas of antelope brush habitat in the Okanagan.

Of the nine per cent of this ecosystem that remains relatively undisturbed, over half lies within the reserve of the Osoyoos Indian Band. More than twenty-three species of animals and plants currently at risk—including western rattlesnakes, burrowing owls and the antelope brush itself—call the area home. By developing what was then called the Desert & Heritage Centre, the Band was both sharing and protecting a delicate resource.

Our young interpreter leads us along a newly gravelled pathway (designed to accommodate disabled visitors) into the arid landscape. She stops to point out the lavender coloured blossoms of mariposa lilies, explaining that her ancestors called them nodding onion and used them for cooking. "They really do taste like green onions," she says. I'm willing to take her word for it.

But there is something I can't help experiencing for myself.

At a Glance

The Nk'Mip Desert Cultural Centre is part of a destination complex created by the Osoyoos Indian Band that includes Nk'Mip Cellars, North America's first aboriginal owned and operated winery; Spirit Ridge Vineyard Resort & Spa; the Passa Tempo restaurant at Spirit Ridge; the 9-hole Sonora Dunes Golf Course; and Nk'Mip RV Park. To reach the Nk'Mip Desert Cultural Centre from downtown Osoyoos, take Hwy 3 east over the bridge. Turn left on 45th Street and follow the signs to Nk'Mip Resort. For information on hours, tour schedules and events, visit www.nkmip.com.

Summer dwelling in the recreated village of the Okanagan (Syilx) people at Nk'Mip Desert Cultural Centre.

Walking that dry trail is like being in a day spa where someone has a heavy hand with the essential oils. No wonder the Okanagan people still burn sage smudge sticks as a spiritual practice. The scent is intense. Shelley shows us the difference between sage and antelope brush, which looked pretty much interchangeable to my untrained eye until she points out the darker green of the antelope brush, then the difference is obvious.

Pausing by a stand of ponderosas, she tells how her people used the versatile pine—needles good for basket-making, pine nuts for pounding into flour, pitch mixed with bear grease as an antiseptic and, on its own, a zesty chewing gum (definitely taking her word on that one).

At the end of the trail we come upon a recreated Okanagan village. Crouching through the entrance of a winter pit house, it's a relief to gather in the relative cool as Shelley describes the ancient social structure of the Okanagan (Syilx) Peoples. With no elected leadership or hierarchy, status was based on knowledge. Women were held in high esteem because they knew where and when to find the staple berry and root crops.

Nk'Mip Desert Cultural Centre, Osoyoos.

The pit house where we stand was constructed by band youth using only the kind of tools that were available to their ancestors. While the project took twice as long as anticipated to complete, Shelley says the builders came away with new understanding and respect for the old ways. It's a small house—a single-family dwelling that would have been used by a new family starting out. Across the clearing stands a larger unit. Typically, around thirty people lived in each of these winter dwellings that were built in a cluster to take advantage of the social time of year.

In summer, when families packed up and scattered to fishing, hunting and picking sites, they lived in portable mat teepees. The village also features one of these along with an authentic sweat lodge.

While the little cluster of structures remains an important feature of the overall Nk'Mip experience, it's somewhat overshadowed now by the stunning facility that opened in 2006.

Built into a hillside and topped with a grass roof, the Nk'Mip Desert Cultural Centre seamlessly blends with the environment. Its façade mimics nature with rammed-earth construction where dirt, pigment, water and a bit of cement was pounded into forms to produce textured layers that echo the look of the mountains behind.

The exhibits are equally creative. One display showcases the artistic flowering of band children in the 1930s and 1940s under the tute-

Holly Peacock sings
her family's song.

Decorative beadwork on
display at the Nk'Mip Desert
Cultural Centre, Osoyoos.

lage of Tony Walsh, a forward thinking white teacher. A six-minute multi-sensory presentation, featuring the voice of an elder and images on four plasma screens, evokes a sense of winter life in a kekuli. Coyote the Transformer leads a journey of discovery via an original movie in the eighty-seat Chaptik Legend Theatre and the Critter Corner provides a window on local wildlife and the band's endangered rattler research (chapter five).

Biologists host talks in the outdoor Living Lands Gallery where metal, rock and water sculptures depict the daily life of a hunter-gatherer people and their close ties with nature. You can dig into a demonstration archeology site, peek inside a bat box and listen to stories in a tule mat teepee. From here, self-guided and guided walks follow gravel pathways through the desert to the Okanagan village.

There's always the chance of spotting some wildlife. The area is posted with reminders to watch for rattlers, though I've never spotted one without the help of a biologist (also in chapter five). But I did once come upon a mule deer calmly browsing in the village.

On my most recent visit, I follow a different interpreter, Holly Peacock, whose stories are as compelling as Shelley's. And when she pulls out a drum, I stand transfixed with the others in my group as she begins a steady soft beat.

"The song is owned by the family," she says, "a travelling song or for good fortune. Others must have permission to use it. This song reminds me of summers with my grandparents, riding and leading a pack horse up to Snowy Mountain."

She sings in a quiet voice, the beat of the drum barely audible, the rhythm of the chanted words like an easy ride along a trail. When her voice dies away, she pauses for a moment. "I almost cry every time I sing it," she says, "thinking of my grandfather."

That's the point of the Nk'Mip centre, thinking of all the grandfathers and grandmothers, of their lives and their relationship with the animals and plants and the land—of our relationships with each other. As Okanagan First Nation member Brenda Baptiste puts it, "For us, this is a centre for transformation. People come here to learn about our culture, but by the time they leave, we've challenged them to think about who they are and their own heritage."

Mural Medley

IF A PICTURE IS WORTH A THOUSAND WORDS, we've got some pretty chatty walls in the Okanagan. My interest in valley murals developed from an assignment to cover a downtown revitalization project under way in Vernon.

In an alley behind Jubilee Park, I discover a paint-splattered young woman on a scaffold brushing colour onto the rough wall. Lead artist Michelle Loughery keeps working as we talk, explaining that the multi-year cooperative project involves teams of local young people in need of a fresh start. Working under her direction, they do much of the painting and learn some valuable life-skills along the way.

Almost anywhere you look in downtown Vernon, a larger-than-life character from the early days of BC's oldest incorporated city outside the Lower Mainland will be looking back. Currently twenty-five historic murals depict the people and events that shaped the modern community. Michelle says heritage photographs inspired much of the chronicle that begins with the First Nations. It includes a tribute to Catherine Schubert, the indefatigable first white woman to travel overland from eastern Canada to BC. Captain Short's rowboat ferry service is there along with firemen and sternwheeler steamships, Vernon's steam laundry and the first airplane constructed in Vernon—built from a kit by a pair of teenagers, Eldon Seymore and Jim Duddle. The murals capture family life, street scenes, the orchard industry and a military presence that began in 1909 with the first cavalry training camp in the province.

At a Glance

The best concentrations of murals in the Okanagan are in Vernon and Lumby, although other communities have a sprinkling. Maps and details on individual murals in Vernon are available online at www.vernonmurals.ca and at the Visitor Centre. For the same information, to join guided tours or to pick up an MP3 player for a self-guided tour, stop by the Downtown Vernon Association in the historic train station on 29th Street. To learn about the Lumby murals, follow the link at www.monasheetour-sm.com to the mural page or drop into the Visitor Centre.

A number of murals are easy to spot as you drive through town on Highway 97, but you'll get more out of a guided tour. Let your human conductor fill in the backstories or rent an MP3 player and explore at your own pace. Maps are also available online and around town. It takes about thirty to forty-five minutes to complete the two-kilometre tour.

Just twenty-minutes to the east, Lumby is the latest entrant into the valley wall-art scene. When two sawmills closed, threatening the community's very existence, it was clear that the economy needed diversification. Turning the village into an outdoor art gallery and visual museum has given tourists another reason to visit the burg that marks the transition between the Okanagan Valley and Monashee Mountains.

Michelle again played a pivotal role. While she herself painted works like *Lumby Looking East* featuring Moses Lumby, the Government Agent in Vernon who lent his name to the village, others reflect her role as teacher and facilitator. *Country Outing*—picturing Will and Birdie Shields in their Model T car—is a prime example. Completed over the winter of 2000/2001, this "workshop mural" is the result of the combined effort of eleven other artists painting under her tutelage and direction.

Along with commemorating people of significance like the Bessette Family, the Lumby collection offers a glimpse into the economic history and ecology of the area. Within the space of a short village walk, you'll meet boxing champ Alphonse Chabot and the 1913 hockey team; learn about crosscut logging, Bluesprings Ranch and miners at Cherry Creek; see oxen building a road and wolves of the Monashee. But possibly the most striking work runs the length of the Legion wall. *Lest We Forget*—an arresting reminder of Canada's role both in combat and peacekeeping—seems particularly poignant today.

Further south in the Okanagan, the murals are less concentrated. In Peachland local Rotarians spearheaded a project to cover the retaining wall at the south end of the downtown beach area next to the museum. To ensure historical accuracy on a work that depicts the past, present and future of the village, lead artist Robyn Lake got help from the Kelowna museum and a local historian. Fundraising got a boost when one Rotary member offered to make a donation in memory of a recent-

Lead artist Michelle Loughery and assistant painting *In Memory*, Vernon Heritage Murals.

ly deceased pet. When others saw the black spaniel being painted into the scene, they too wanted a shot at immortality. While maintaining full artistic control, Robyn was able to incorporate many local faces and images.

Summerland hosts a tribute to the orchard and packing industry on the wall of its packing house and Osoyoos has unveiled a mural on the community centre, dedicated to the many Portuguese who settled in the valley particularly in the 1960s and contributed enormously to the development of those same industries.

Penticton's murals centre on the downtown core. Some, dating back to the early 1990s, were produced by Grade 10 art students from the McNicholl Park Jr. Secondary School. More recent additions include a work depicting current and past uses of Nanaimo Hall, off Main Street; lake steamers and the Kettle Valley Railway on Lakeshore Drive; and on Ellis, a mural commemorating the Penticton Vee's hockey team, which won the world championship in 1955. You'll notice references to Germany, where the game was played, and the defeated Russian team (yes!). While a few more murals contribute to the Colourful Front Street theme, my no-contest favourite brings me full-circle to another alley. To see the collection of fanciful characters on the back wall of the Bookshop, take the pedestrian walkway from Main Street and turn right.

Christine Pilgrim as Grace Mackie at Mackie Lake House, near Vernon. Facing page: S.S. Sicamous, Penticton.

Chapter 9
History Rocks

YOU CAN TELL FROM THE LENGTH OF THIS CHAPTER
that I'm a huge history buff, which is something of a handicap in a
region where European settlement took root only a hundred and fifty
years ago. The Ontario farmhouse where I spent much of my early life
had already sheltered two generations by the time Father Pandosy set
up his mission in present-day Kelowna—and by European and Asian
standards, a century-and-a-half is barely a blip on the timeline. Of
course, First Nations history in the region reaches back thousands
of years and I feel a pang about my enjoyment of the settlers' stories,
knowing that their triumphs came at the expense of a whole people's
way of life. No doubt that's part of the reason that I compartmentalize
the two in my own mind, preferring to think of the First Nations
legacy in terms of culture and a connection with the environment,
which is how I've presented the material. So this chapter relates
my experience with attractions that commemorate the origins of
modern Okanagan society in terms of post-contact settlement.

Mackie Lake House

"DON'T RAISE YOUR PINKIE, DEAR, else people will think you're the plumber's daughter."

Grace Mackie (a.k.a. actress/interpreter Christine Pilgrim) smiles graciously, sipping delicately from a fragile gold-rimmed cup. We're seated at a damask covered table on the capacious veranda of Mackie Lake House overlooking Kalamalka Lake. Small pink roses stand in a dainty cut glass vase flanked by a plate of trimmed cucumber sandwiches, another of fresh scones and a pot of fruit preserves. A tray of sherbet glasses filled with strawberries, peaches and clotted cream waits on the sideboard.

I instantly drop the offending digit—*who knew these things*. Besides, I don't even like tea (strictly a java girl) and anyway, it's all her fault. If Christine weren't playing the lady of the house so convincingly, I wouldn't be speaking in hushed tones, carefully dabbing crumbs from the corners of my lips—or elevating my little finger.

But the rebuke is a small price to pay for an entertaining afternoon. On set dates between May and September, this gracious arts and crafts house, built in 1910 and owned by the Mackie family from 1945 until it was bequeathed to a foundation when Paddy Mackie died in 1999, is open for tours and tea.

Hosted by "Grace Mackie"—who shows off her favourite features of the surprisingly well preserved period interior; divulges little secrets ("We bought the Sheraton sideboard second hand, you know"); plays a running game of which-is-the-Jane Austen teapot; and breaks your heart with the tragic stories of losing three of her four sons—it's a rare chance to live, just a little, of an earlier time in the Okanagan, not to mention perfecting your tea drinking skills.

At a Glance

Mackie Lake House is located at 7804 Kidston Road in Coldstream (south of Vernon). It is open for guided tours on a limited basis from June through August. Book reservations online or call 250.545.1019. Dates for Tours & Tea With Grace Mackie (a.k.a. Christine Pilgrim) are listed at www.mackiehouse.ca.

Fintry

ON THE FIRST DAY OF HIS FIRST TRIP to the Okanagan, I drove Bruce north from Kelowna on Westside Road. I calculated that this two-lane string of blind curves opening onto jaw-dropping lake views would be enough to convince the man that he should move to the valley (in case my personal charms weren't incentive enough).

We stopped for a picnic on a grassy hillside overlooking Okanagan Lake then drove on to Fintry, one of the best historic sites in the region. Nature blessed the rich Fintry delta, spreading beyond the triple waterfall where Shorts Creek takes a dramatic plunge—and a laird made it his home.

James Cameron Dun-Waters, wealthy publisher of the Glasgow Herald, bought what was then called Shorts Point in 1909. He heard about it through the old boys network on a hunting trip to the Kootenays with Governor General Lord Grey. The canny Scot scooped up the property for $22,500 (over $400,000 in today's dollars, but still an amazing bargain) and renamed it for his ancestral home.

Too bad he wasn't around a few decades earlier or Dun-Waters could have had Fintry for an even more unbelievable price. Captain Thomas D. Shorts got the best deal. The first European to pre-empt the land, which had long been known by fur traders and Hudson's Bay men, found it made a perfect base for his *rowboat* ferry business. Eventually, Shorts was caught short (financially) and looked to unload his holding. Yet even after dropping the tab to a laughable $75, there were still no takers.

At a Glance

Fintry Provincial Park encompasses three hundred and sixty hectares of the former Fintry estate. It is located thirty-four kilometres north of Kelowna and forty-nine kilometres south of Vernon on the west side of Okanagan Lake off Westside Road. Online details at www.env.gov.bc.ca/bcparks. The campground operates from April 1 to October 15. Reserve campsites at www.discovercamping.ca. The octagonal barn and manor house are open for tours during the summer months. You can climb the stairs to view Fintry Falls any time you have the energy.

Enter a pair of English remittance men. When they inquired about the price, Shorts sized them up and brazenly suggested $4,000. To the wealthy adventurers this seemed reasonable enough. Shorts took the money and ran. Ironically, the two Englishmen went home and never returned. The property fell into decay until Dun-Waters showed up with his chequebook and developed Fintry into a luxurious estate. Today, it's a provincial park and hopping busy on the hot August afternoon of our visit.

It looks to us as if every one of the campsites is occupied and I can't spot an empty mooring beyond the old-growth cottonwoods that rim the two-kilometre sandy shoreline. I set about cajoling my fella into taking a full-on look at the waterfalls. Even in late summer there's enough water cascading over the thirty-five metre drop to make quite a show and in Dun-Waters' day it was sufficient to irrigate forty hectares of apple orchards and provide hydroelectric power to the estate.

"It's only about three hundred steps," I wheedle, "and there are platforms every twenty or thirty steps. You can catch your breath … And think of the photo ops," I add, hoping to clinch the deal by ruthlessly striking his Achilles heel. "At the top you literally hang out over the gorge."

That gets him—though it comes dangerously close to foiling my long-term romantic aspirations. We make it to the top, all right. But I probably don't need to spell out the details of that climb on a typically broiling Okanagan summer afternoon. I admit to a certain level of alarm at the shade of puce that suffuses Bruce's face and it takes a couple of days for him to fully rehydrate. The fact that we're still together speaks volumes about his forgiving nature and since that day Bruce has shown a marked reluctance to take any of my hiking suggestions at face value. Go figure.

He does gamely admit that Shorts Creek canyon is impressive and the waterfalls worth the climb (in spring or autumn). Of course, we don't spot any of the California bighorn sheep that find safe habitat in the surrounding hills or the deer that use the area for winter range. They're all bedded down in the shade or long gone to the cooler high country. But he does cast an appraising eye at the creek downstream from the falls with thoughts of kokanee and rainbows, no doubt just as Dun-Waters did when he first saw the property.

It's not that hard to put the trials of the climb behind us as we check out Fintry's other attractions. The laird's packing house is among the last of these once common working spaces that were serviced by the sternwheelers of the lake. And the octagonal dairy barn is unique. Dun-Waters actually employed an architect to design the space for his prized Ayrshire herd with the silo in the middle and inward facing milking stations so that his cows could be fed centrally.

Dun-Waters housed himself equally comfortably. While the manor house is not particularly imposing by Scottish baronial standards, it bespeaks an elegant time. Its owner was well known for maintaining good taste and social standards even though miles of forest and water isolated the estate. His dining room featured the best in wild game and farm produce served on proper china. Beneath its floorboards was Dun-Waters' private cellar, stocked with great wines and Scotch whisky, labelled Laird of Fintry.

Constructed of stone and local timber, the sprawling bungalow we tour is not as Dun-Waters built it for his first wife, Alice. Little more than a year after her death in 1924, the manor house burned. Workers rescued only some of the furnishings (although the liquor cellar escaped), but the laird rebuilt, this time finishing the trophy room he'd started before the fire.

Among the antlers and animal heads stands the Kodiak bear Dun-Waters shot in Alaska, posed in a special closet he called The Grotto. Bruce loves this part; but I can't help thinking he'd like it even better if there'd been some samples left from that cellar.

The fact that we can visit this terrific remnant of Okanagan history is a testament to the volunteering spirit in the valley. In the year 2000, the Friends of Fintry Society was founded and its members continue to pour thousands of hours into restoration, maintenance, fundraising and guiding people like us through the Dun-Waters legacy.

Fintry manor, now protected in Fintry Provincial Park, was built by James Cameron Dun-Waters.

Architect-designed octagonal barn with central silo and inward facing milking stations allowed Dun-Waters' prized Ayrshires to be fed centrally.

Historic O'Keefe Ranch

"THE BX IS COMING," shouts a little boy running along the boardwalk toward us. "I saw it around the bend by the church." Excitement ripples through the small crowd gathered in front of the general store. The thrill running through my bones is straight out of the 1880s.

O'Keefe Ranch was the first stagecoach depot in the Okanagan. Bernard Express coaches, drawn by horses bred for the job at the nearby BX Ranch, were the settlers' most important link with the outside world. I've read about the isolation of early ranchers and tried to imagine what it was like for Mary Ann O'Keefe after she left her father's prosperous Ontario farm to share this life with her husband Cornelius. I've toured the two-storey log home he built for her in 1876 and the lavish Victorian that replaced it ten years later.

Yet nothing in a book or a building or even my mind's eye compares with the reaction I feel to those clattering hooves, the pungent smell of horse sweat and the mile-wide grin on the driver's sun-weathered face as he reigns in his team and the big box on wheels creaks to a stop before us. In that moment I know, if only in the smallest fleeting way, how Mary Ann felt when she caught sight of the coach bearing news from back east and maybe a bolt of cloth for new baby clothes.

The BX is no longer a regular feature at O'Keefe, but the ranch still hosts the annual Cowboy Festival where people get a chance to personally experience cowboy culture and every day there's an opportunity to see aspects of a working cattle ranch. Kids whose closest encounter with a live farm animal involves the Discovery Channel can't get enough of the barnyard critters. Me either.

At a Glance

O'Keefe Ranch is located twelve kilometres north of Vernon in the Spallumcheen Valley. Follow Hwy 97 past Swan Lake and take the Kamloops turnoff. The entrance is about four kilometres from the junction. The ranch is open daily, 9 a.m. to 5 p.m. from late-April through mid-October. The Ranch Gift Shop is open during the season while the Cattlemen's Club Restaurant operates year round. For hours of operation and a full schedule of seasonal events including the Victorian Christmas visit www.okeeferanch.bc.ca.

(for reference only – not to scale)

Other main attractions show how the ranch was very much a self-contained community with its own post office (in operation before Vernon's), a blacksmith shop and St. Anne's church. One of the oldest Roman Catholic churches in the Okanagan, it served parishioners from 1889 to the 1950s.

The general store, where we waited for the BX stagecoach, opened in 1872. Stocked with a boggling array of antique merchandise, it's my mom's favourite spot at the ranch. She loves to take on the costumed interpreters in a Jeopardy-style challenge of what's this. They never stump her. And she never leaves without a little bag of the penny candy they sell.

Some of the buildings, like the Schubert House (owned by the son of Catherine Schubert, the only woman among the Overlanders who trekked into the valley in 1862 from the east), have been moved from nearby locations to cluster at the historic site. Others remain where

St. Anne's church at O'Keefe Ranch, Vernon, is one of the oldest Roman Catholic churches in the Okanagan.

they were built. All provide a peek at the life and times of the migrants who made their living from ranching.

You see implement and carriage sheds, the meat and dairy (ice) house, the cabin shared by Chinese cooks and the cowboys' bunkhouse. Every structure was used—and used again. The first building on the ranch, shelter for Cornelius and his partners when they preempted their land, became the milk house. Ranch hands and the family governess and her husband lived in the O'Keefe's first log home, moved to make way for construction of "the mansion."

Though built during Mary Ann's life, this house now reflects a later period of affluence. The luxury-loving tastes of Cornelius' second wife, Elizabeth, are highlighted in its extravagant Victorian dining room and parlour, while her more practical side surfaces in the simple second-floor sewing room and nursery.

The Greenhow Museum (named for Thomas Greenhow, O'Keefe's early partner and later neighbour) occupies a small house built in the 1940s. It contains ranching and cowboy exhibits along with displays illustrating the story of the Okanagan People. A model railway takes up the second floor.

O'Keefe is one of those historic attractions that don't cause kids to roll their eyes. They can do lots of running and touching—always popular. Families are welcome to spread a picnic under the maple trees and make a day of it. Me, I just want to ride that coach again.

Mom waves from the BX stagecoach at O'Keefe Ranch, Vernon.

Okanagan Heritage Museum

I'M SO ASHAMED. In sixteen years of living in and around Kelowna, I had never set foot in the Okanagan Heritage Museum. Others yes—Penticton, Peachland, Vernon, Osoyoos—I'd even checked out Kelowna's satellite venues: the Okanagan Military Museum, the BC Orchard Industry Museum and the BC Wine Museum. But somehow, the building I drove by a couple of times a week, never edged onto my to-do list.

It's small comfort to know that I'm not alone in my shame. Bet if you do one of those mic-in-the-face man-in-the-street ambushes and ask when your victim last checked out the museum, most people will look at their shoes and say: "The next time will be my first."

Even Betty, the bubbly volunteer who jumps up from her seat behind the info desk to greet me when I finally make a visit, has to admit that she'd never walked through the front door until she applied for her job—despite working for eons in the federal building across the street. Late start or not, Betty turned into a real booster. "You're going to love this one," she beams, indicating the temporary and special exhibition area with a Vanna White sweep of the hand.

We Are Métis is the current display and features the work of Dennis Weber. "He's a very talented artist—a very gentle man," she says. "I think you'll find the exhibit quite unique." To say the least.

Not two steps past her desk I'm bowled over by the black and white image of a First Nations boy. Hung on a red background, the stark contrast of graphite on PVC plastic depicting a youngster waiting to make

At a Glance

The Okanagan Heritage Museum is located at the corner of Queensway Avenue and Ellis Street in Kelowna. Next door, the Okanagan Military Museum occupies space in the Memorial Arena. One block north, at 1304 Ellis St., the historic Laurel Packinghouse hosts both the British Columbia Orchard Industry Museum and the British Columbia Wine Museum & VQA Wine Shop. From Harvey Avenue (Hwy 97), turn north on Ellis Street and continue through downtown to Kelowna's Cultural District. Admission is by donation. Visit www.kelownamuseum.ca for seasonal hours.

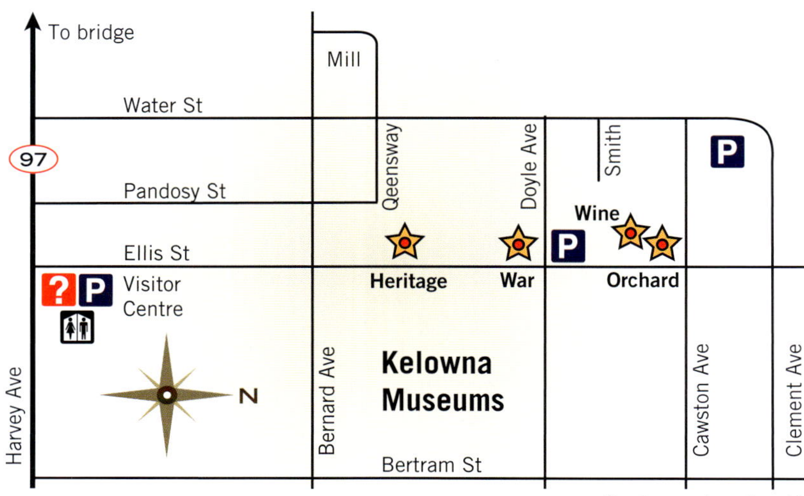

(for reference only – not to scale)

his entrance at the Calgary Stampede stops me cold. Weber specializes in portraits, usually with a First Nations theme.

Eventually, I tear my eyes from the child's face and move on. A lively fiddle tune defies the subdued tone of the dimly lit gallery where spotlights punctuate the beauty of treasures in glass cases—a bear claw necklace, antique beads, moccasins decorated with tufted moose hair—created by a variety of artists.

Deeper in the museum, where displays feature exhibits from the extensive permanent collection of First Nations artifacts, I'm drawn to the pleasing shapes and designs of woven baskets. For millennia, women crafted these everyday essentials, decorating them with wild rye grass and cherry bark and weaving in their signature designs. But by the 1890s the increasing European influence was impacting traditional techniques and some aniline dyes were replacing natural sources like mud, berries, lichen and ochre. As well, new shapes evolved for new purposes such as sewing baskets.

At John McDougal's Trading Post I have to bend low through a doorway that barely reaches my shoulder to step into the source of the revolution. Physically moved—lock, stock and flour barrel—from its original site in Kelowna's Guisachan area, this Hudson's Bay Company cabin dates to 1861. Trade goods from tea to tobacco, water jugs to whisky flasks, beads to blankets are stacked on rough shelves anchored to the squared log walls and piled on the twelve-inch floor planks (I measure with my foot).

Close by, the story of Father Pandosy and his mission (more on this later in the chapter) fills a glass case and makes sense in the context of local history. What baffles me is the Ethnography Gallery with its pots and talismans from Central and South America, Asia, Oceania and Africa. While interesting in themselves, I personally find its placement detracts from the flow of the Okanagan story and would really prefer to see it in some other part of the museum. But that's just me.

What I do enjoy is glimpsing the lifestyle of the sternwheeler era, with its gracious lakeshore hotels, cricket matches and fishing regattas, and peeking through the green-trimmed window of a white clapboard storefront into a totally different world, a world I didn't know once flourished here.

Between 1900 and 1965, Kelowna hosted a mini-Chinatown that numbered five hundred souls at its zenith in the 1930s. In the two blocks bounded by Water and Abbott streets, its buildings faced the alley between Harvey and Leon. Most of the predominantly male population, drawn mainly from Kwangtung province, came first as miners then moved on to help build the CPR. Later arrivals laid tracks for the Kettle Valley Railway and contributed immensely to the orchard industry, building hundreds of miles of flumes and ditches, then working in the orchards—usually through labour bosses.

First Nations basket displayed at the Okanagan Heritage Museum, Kelowna.

A glimpse of Kelowna's former Chinatown in the Wong family store, Okanagan Heritage Museum, Kelowna.

Passage of the Chinese Exclusion Act in 1923, which halted further immigration and prevented men from bringing their wives to Canada, spelled the eventual demise of the community. By 1960, fewer than sixty people and only two buildings remained.

Preserved in the museum is the front section of a store owned by the Wong family who lived upstairs and, as I can see through the window, sold ginseng and herbs and dried duck eggs in the shop below. I move on, but the images and story stick with me.

The rest of the exhibits are great. Whoever got the bright idea of creating a basement filled with the detritus of generations as a way to display everything from push mowers (so old they're new again) to gramophones and snowshoes, was a genius. The 1908 Motor Buggy is cool and I get a kick out of the 1920s panorama painting of Kelowna, created for the Gibson Catlett Real Estate Company. Some things never change.

A separate gallery off the entrance area (where Betty is now busy with new arrivals) is clearly designed to send shivers up small spines. Beaver skulls, dinosaur heads and one really big grizzly produce just the right thrill factor. For me, not so much. But I do enjoy checking out the pine needle art and historic photos in the gift shop.

This isn't a large museum, but it's laid out with the optical trickery of a Japanese garden. It seems bigger—to contain more. And I'm still thinking about that little shop in Chinatown.

Pandosy Mission

DRIVE BY THE SMALL CLUSTER OF LOG STRUCTURES on Benvoulin Road in Kelowna and you could be forgiven for not recognizing the site as a watershed in Okanagan history. The unprepossessing little park contains remnants of the Immaculate Conception Mission—known to us as the Pandosy Mission. Here, over the fall and winter of 1859-1860, Oblate fathers Charles Pandosy and Pierre Richard established the first European settlement in the valley.

The mission's priests and brothers saw to the spiritual needs of both settlers and converted First Nations people and it became an important cultural, social and religious centre. The Oblate fathers opened the first school and church in the valley. They also developed a thriving farm operation with cattle, grain and vegetables and planted the Okanagan's first fruit trees and grape vines. The mission flourished while its dynamic founder lived. But when Pandosy died in 1891 it began a downhill slide, finally closing in 1896. A decade later, the property was sold.

Soon after my arrival in the Okanagan, I drag my eleven-year-old daughter along for our first foray into local history. I have to give her credit for feigning some interest in the weathered buildings. And she's pretty discreet with the eye rolling when we encounter the mannequins stiffly representing Father Pandosy, John MacDougall, the first permanent trader (who's cabin is now in the Okanagan Heritage Museum), and his aboriginal wife. Let's just say that the visit is a qualified success. If only I'd known about the missing body.

It wasn't until Bruce moved here many years later and began researching a story on the mission that this macabre tale surfaced.

At a Glance

The Pandosy Mission is located at 3685 Benvoulin Road in Kelowna. It is jointly administered by the Okanagan Historical Society and the Roman Catholic Church. A good brochure is available at the Kelowna Visitor Centre. A caretaker lives onsite and the grounds are open to the public for self-guided tours from dawn to dusk from mid-April to mid-October. Admission is by donation.

I'll let him take it from here.

"When they opened the grave, they were sure they had finally found Father Pandosy," he says. "The man's remains were dressed in the long black robe that Pandosy favoured and the height of the occupant tallied with the records noting Pandosy as a big man—nearly two metres tall. So why was Pandosy not where everyone thought he should be?"

Bruce explains that this wasn't the first time something connected with the Pandosy Mission had nearly gone missing. "Before the restoration, there was a brief period when the mission itself seemed to be temporarily misplaced. In the early 1950s not many people knew where the remaining buildings were located and they were only days away from being razed by the owner of the property where they sat."

Enter a writer named Norma Carter who ran across the story in 1954 and immediately contacted the Oblates to suggest restoration. Her letter intrigued Father O'Grady, head of the English-speaking Oblates in Canada, enough that he hopped a plane for Kelowna to inspect the mission site.

Bruce says, "O'Grady was met by Lawrence Guichon from the Kelowna Historical Society who was to act as his guide. To what must surely have been his embarrassment, Guichon couldn't remember exactly where the mission was and had to turn to a colleague, H.C.S. 'Shorty' Collett to show them the way."

The four remaining buildings were slated to be torched in just a few weeks. O'Grady jumped into action, negotiating a $1,200 deal with the landowner, then convincing a friend and local lawyer to put up the money. Part of the deal saw the Oblates assume responsibility for surveying and fencing.

Over the next three years, lean-tos on the grounds were knocked down and the four acres comprising today's mission site were cleared of weeds and refuse. In the fall of 1957 another Oblate, Father James Mul-

Christien House, one of the heritage buildings preserved at Pandosy Mission in Kelowna.

vihill, landed in Kelowna with orders to restore the buildings. O'Grady wanted them ready for re-dedication the following year. Bruce says, "Mulvihill made it happen with the help of Jack Bedford, Grand Knight of the Knights of Columbus, and his lodge." On June 15, 1958, four of the original buildings were re-dedicated, the brothers' house, chapel, root house and barn.

Over time more historic buildings were added to the collection. In the 1970s, the Christien home, a log cabin dating from the turn of the 20th century was moved from its original location near the present Kelowna International Airport. It took two days to accomplish the transport. The blacksmith shop and John MacDougall house were added later, bringing the number of period buildings that you can visit to seven.

"But Father Pandosy himself was missing," says Bruce. "Not only was he missing, but the graveyard where he was buried had also gone astray."

Enter James Baker, an Okanagan College archeology instructor who began looking for Pandosy's final resting place in 1983. Helped by two Simon Fraser archeology students he set out to establish the exact location of the graveyard.

"After excavating two trenches, the team located the impressions of postholes from the cemetery fencing just west of the current mission site at the Ramponi vegetable stand on Gordon Road. Now," says Bruce, "the trick was to find Pandosy without disturbing too many of his neighbours."

Records indicated that Pandosy had been buried alongside two other priests. They also reported he was entombed with an iron crucifix, a claim supported by the fact that Pandosy is pictured wearing a large cross on the front of his cassock.

"Easy enough," says Bruce. "The three archeologists combed the grounds with a metal detector. But unlike Indiana Jones, they came up empty handed." It wasn't until they began excavating gravesites that they finally found the lost priest. Instead of lying with his colleagues, Pandosy was resting comfortably with his parishioners, and he wasn't holding the iron cross.

"Now," says Bruce, "The only remaining mystery is: Where's Pandosy's cross?"

Kettle Valley Steam Train

TWO LONG—ONE SHORT—ONE LONG. Steam engine No. 3 announces her approach to Prairie Valley Station with the jaunty call of her whistle. Along with everybody else on the platform, from pre-teens to pensioners (my mom and dad among them), I lean out for a better look as she puffs into view through a stand of ponderosa pine. The shining black engine wheezes to a stop, belching plumes as white as the pillowy clouds drifting in the blue morning sky. I feel a tingle. *We're going for a train ride.*

Brakemen in pinstripe overalls spring into action coupling the 1924 Shay locomotive to the waiting cars and blue-uniformed conductors begin welcoming us aboard. People with reservations for the two open-sided observation cars stream toward the front and back of the train while the rest of us find our seats in the day coaches sandwiched between. Our car, with its alternating rows of blue and red seats, smells faintly old, a bit dusty, quite authentic.

Another whistle blast signals our departure. "All abo-o-ard," calls the conductor on a rising note. The car lurches as engine No. 3 takes up the load. Ch-----ch----ch---ch--ch-ch-ch-ch-ch …. A skifter of steam drifts through the open door and we slowly gather momentum.

Every face wears a grin. We're only setting off on a thirty-two kilometre round trip, but I can tell from the look on my mom's face that, for some, the journey will take them a lot farther. Every one of us is just as thrilled as the passengers who relied on the Kettle Valley Railway from 1916 to 1964.

At a Glance

The Kettle Valley Steam Train departs from the Prairie Valley Station at 18404 Bathville Road, Summerland. The Trout Creek Trading Co. gift shop is located in the station and stocks a selection of railway-themed souvenirs, pioneer toys, books and clothing. Next to the station is a large covered picnic area. Trains operate from mid-May to mid-October with two departures most days. Special event trains include Mother's Day, Father's Day, Christmas and several Great Train Robberies. Reservations recommended for regularly scheduled runs and required for special events, phone 1.877.494.8424. For details visit www.kettlevalleyrail.org.

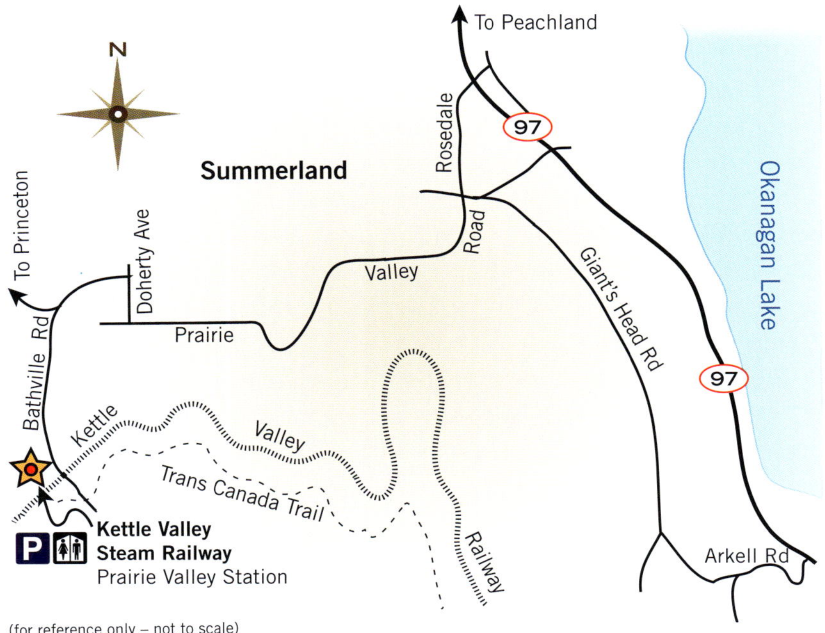

(for reference only – not to scale)

Known as McCulloch's Wonder because of the tremendous obstacles and difficult terrain the chief engineer had to conquer in building the line, this steel highway connected Kootenay mining country with the Coast and provided a vital link for the developing Okanagan fruit industry.

The last freight passed through here in 1989 and most of the track has since been pulled up. But a dedicated group of local citizens fought hard to retain the small section from Trout Creek Bridge to Faulder. Conductor Bill Baker, a retiree who says that "sitting down and playing cards would drive me crazy," is one of many volunteers and a handful of seasonal workers who do everything from repairing track to scrounging rolling stock.

Fellow conductor Keith Franklin provides commentary over the PA as we skirt the green orchards and neat horse paddocks of Prairie Valley and steam toward the hulking flank of Giant's Head Mountain. Keith explains that CPR president Thomas Shaughnessy, founder of Summerland, once owned the entire valley and *encouraged* other railway executives to purchase orchards from his development company.

"There's a dog," shouts one of the four little girls in facing seats two rows up. Three heads swivel to follow her pointing finger. Okay, so the kids aren't as interested in long-dead executives as spotting items to complete the scavenger hunt sheet that brakeman Joe Burt, a high school student and three-summer KVR veteran, distributed. But they will remember this special ride in their own way and someday maybe reflect on a unique experience that, for their grandparents, was a part of everyday life.

For passengers like my mom and dad, the trip is filled with nostalgia. Like our conductor, they grew up in the era of steam. "I can't believe it when people tell me this is their first ride on a train," says Keith, adding with a grin, "Makes me remember how old I am."

A rhythmic clanging briefly filters into the car as we pass a level crossing. A short string of vehicles wait for us to pass and hands stretch out to wave us on our way. At Canyon View siding, while the crew waters up the engine we pile out for a look at the trestle bridge that spans Trout Creek, 72.5 metres above the canyon floor. This is one of McCulloch's major achievements. The engineer personally resur-

Kettle Valley steam train, Summerland.

veyed the canyon when a disagreement erupted over the measurements of the bridge. When completed and lowered into place the seventy-six metre long structure, one of the longest and highest of its kind in North America, was only half-a-centimetre short of a perfect fit. Now that's a wonder.

On the way back I discover that there are some pretty wonderful characters working up front as well. Brad, the man in the right-hand seat, was the youngest steam engineer in Canada and he's teamed up with a fireman named Barb. When we arrive at the station she invites me into the engine for a look around. Climbing into the cramped cab, I'm smothered by the blanket of radiant heat. She opens the firebox door and it's suddenly Dante's Inferno.

Barb, who started out as a volunteer in the office so her son could ride the train, explains that it's her job to adjust the injector lever and water valve as Brad increases or decreases the throttle. She's been the fireman for three years and is just about to qualify as the only female steam engineer in the country.

Since I took that ride into history with my folks, the railway has expanded operations. Engine No. 3 has been joined by No. 3716, a 2-8-0 locomotive (you train buffs will know what that means) built in 1912 in Montreal. It worked a full career then enjoyed considerable movie fame before joining the Kettle Valley Steam Railway. I guess it's time this grandma introduced another generation to the magic of steam.

Steam engine fireman named Barb.

S.S. Sicamous

I'M A SUCKER FOR ALL THINGS NAUTICAL, so I was pretty excited to discover that I could board the largest remaining sternwheeler in Canada, just down the road in Penticton. I'll admit that it was a little startling to see her moored *in* the beach, but better there than a scrap yard.

Speeding down Hwy 97 it takes some serious imagination to conjure a picture of the Okanagan before the reign of automobiles. The very idea of life before "the bridge" is hard to grasp. In a world of jet travel, light-speed communications and big-box food emporiums, it's tough to wrap your brain around the concept of a fourteen-and-a-half hour trip from Penticton to Okanagan Landing (near Vernon); of waiting on the wharf for the steamer to bring mail, news and gossip; of watching stevedores haul your groceries ashore. But in 1914, that was life.

When the queen of the lake slid down the ways and began her career the big sternwheeler's job was to move people and freight within the valley and to railheads connecting the Okanagan with the outside world.

Commissioned by the Canadian Pacific Railway Company BC Lake and River Service (imagine their letterhead), she was built in Port Arthur, Ontario. It took nineteen rail cars to move her hull and engines to the assembly point at OK Landing Shipyards.

The S.S. Sicamous was not the first sternwheeler to ply the Okanagan, but she was designed to be the most luxurious. Passengers met in elegant public rooms lined in cedar and parquet panelling decorated with Burmese teak. Australian mahogany gleamed from the grand stairway. Silver sparkled on white linen in the light of electric candelabra in the dining room and the ladies' salon was furnished in stylish wicker.

Folks who weren't wild about climbing out of bed in time for the 5:30 a.m. departure (how I can relate) could board in the evening and spend a restful night in one of her thirty-seven staterooms. White-coat-

At a Glance

The largest remaining sternwheeler in Canada, the S.S. Sicamous, is beached at 1099 Lakeshore Drive West, Penticton, in the Okanagan Inland Marine Heritage Park. Visit www.sssicamous.com for hours.

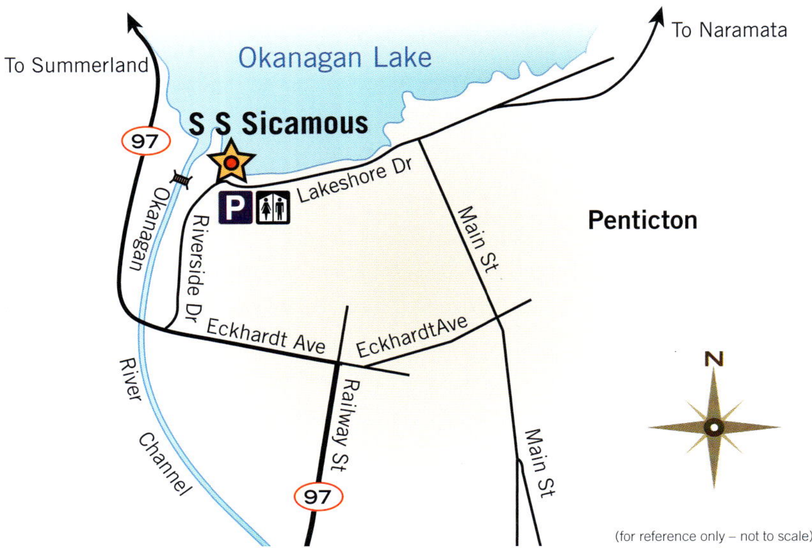

ed stewards served breakfast in the two-story dining room with its surrounding gallery. Food prepared by Chinese cooks in the Deck A galley arrived via dumb waiter.

Between meals, gents gathered in the smoking salon forward. Ladies had their own salon at the stern and an observation lounge above. Historic photos show that when the Sicamous sidled up to shore for one of her fourteen scheduled stops, most passengers crowded on deck, lining the rails to watch the excitement.

Through the Great War, the enormous prosperity of the 1920s and into the lean years of the 30s, the Sicamous was part of the fabric of Okanagan life. But the world was changing. In her twenty-second year, the grand lady was remodelled to reflect hard times and decreased service. Two-thirds of the gallery deck was removed and her deckhead lowered onto the dining room/stern salon. Just a year later, the Sicamous made her last run.

Half-a-century later, the once proud steamship lay derelict. Realizing that an important part of valley history would soon disappear, concerned citizens formed a rescue plan. Since 1988 the S.S. Sicamous Restoration Society has poured thousands of hours and millions of dollars into making her a museum.

You don't have to be a history buff to appreciate what they've accomplished. The first thing you see on the cargo deck as you start the self-guided tour is the vessel's enormous power plant. Her twenty-three-foot-long boiler gobbled seventeen tons of coal each day to maintain a cruising speed of eighteen knots—eighteen knots, that's over thirty-three kilometres an hour!

Passengers actually boarded the Sicamous on Deck B and immediately stopped by the purser's cabin to buy tickets, check in baggage and arrange cabin rentals. All his tools of the trade are laid out in the recreated cabin. The ladies' salon and dining room occupy the same deck, but you have to rely on historic photos to see how splendid this space was before the Sicamous was pared down and the gallery removed.

Along with all the nautical and period artifacts around the ship, it's a surprise to find a reminder of another great achievement of the age of steam onboard. Constructed by the KVR Model Train Club, a huge display depicts the Kettle Valley Railway from Midway to Hope, including a scale model of Penticton in the 1930s with the Sicamous and tug Naramata at dock.

The ship's wheel no longer hangs in the grand stairway, but it is still onboard the S.S. Sicamous, Penticton.

Naramata Heritage Inn

"THE BEST THING FOR THAT BUILDING IS A MATCH," scoffed onlookers when restorations began on the Hotel Naramata.

Built in 1908, the near derelict once stood as the crowning achievement of land developer John Moore Robinson who made his fortune in eastern newspapers and came west during the Klondike gold rush. He had already spearheaded development of Peachland and Summerland and he envisioned Naramata as an ideal location for the "perfect community," calling it "the California of Canada."

Robinson moved his family from Summerland and they lived in a tent house on the grounds during construction (imagine The Donald doing that!). The Hotel Naramata was to be the centrepiece of his plan for a recreation destination to attract vacationers from the Okanagan and beyond. He furnished the gracious California mission-style building with mission furniture and arts and crafts fixtures.

For a time the dream was reality, but through the years his beautiful creation went from hotel to family home to private girls' school. By the 1990s the grand old lady by the lake was a lifeless shell.

It took three tries to convince Norm and Janette Davies to abandon their careers in Vancouver and return to the valley to join in the resuscitation. But they didn't regret the move. "The place is turning out to be exactly what we had in mind from the beginning," said Norm as he showed me around the newly renovated and rechristened Naramata Inn in May 2002. "We had this picture in our head. It is bang on exactly the way we wanted it."

The way they wanted it is authentic and the partners went to extraordinary lengths to achieve their vision. Dark-stained wainscotting, railings, baseboards and beams, beloved of Edwardian designers, contrast with the scrubbed blond-tone fir plank flooring on the first level. As much as possible the layout remains unchanged, except that the original seventeen guest rooms have been reformatted to eleven suites with

At a Glance

The Naramata Heritage Inn & Spa is located at 3625 1st Street in Naramata. For more information visit www.naramatainn.com.

private baths featuring vintage clawfoot tubs. While the rooms are small by North American standards, large windows and high ceilings give an airy feel and each has direct access to the veranda, shaded by lofty American elms.

Attention to detail borders on the fanatical even where the result would be invisible to all but the most knowledgeable observer. Existing brass wall fixtures were rewired and antique radiators rejuvenated. Furniture dates to the period between 1898 and 1912, many pieces still bearing the Ship to Naramata stamp. Instead of replacing worn window casings the double hung sliders were removed, repaired and reinstalled. To replace broken panes, Norm tracked down a San Fransisco importer representing a Greek company that still produced characteristically wavy, pitted, mouth-blown plate glass. Where wood was simply too rotten to save, it was replaced with hundred-year-old lumber salvaged from a building in Chilliwak, BC.

Other materials were recycled. Planking from the second-storey veranda, taken up to make way for paving stones, now forms the wainscotting in the Cobblestone Wine Bar & Restaurant. Building this hideaway in the former cellar/crawl space revealed concrete apparently mixed using coarse Naramata beach sand. Norm ordered that new construction be authentic right down to the bits of sticks and leaves visible in the walls. The result of this painstaking effort is a visitor-friendly heritage retreat and I think old J.M. would be delighted to see people enjoying the 21st century incarnation of his vision.

Naramata Heritage Inn & Spa.

Okanagan Science Centre, Vernon. Facing page: Pumpkin man rescues treed kitty, Davison Orchards, Vernon.

Chapter 10
Family Time

ONE OF THE BENEFITS OF BEING A GRANDMA is freedom from pressure. For me the statement, "Mom, I'm bored" has happily faded to mouldering memory. I've passed the torch (with a powerful sense of justice finally achieved) to my daughter Brandie. How I relish the knowledge that it's her turn to deal with rainy weekends, her responsibility to struggle with spring break, her time to fight the frustration of late August, longing for the liberating sound of the school bell — while I pop in and out the picture on a whim. What fun it is to call up and say, "How be we take Alex to the fair this weekend?" knowing that grandma will be a hero for buying corn dogs (junk food normally off limits), supplying an extra strip of tickets for the midway (grandma's have a special budget that moms and dads can't manage) and willingly standing in line for one more go at petting the baby llama. And when the little tummy starts to churn and the accumulation of activity and excitement inevitably produces a case of the tired crankies, I can cheerily wave good-bye as they head for home. I love family time.

Okanagan Science Centre

I THINK SCIENCE CENTRE AND MENTAL IMAGES of the slick multi-$million extravaganzas in Vancouver and Toronto spring to mind. The Okanagan Science Centre is nothing like either one. In fact, the Vernon version occupies a heritage schoolhouse (built in 1893) in Polson Park. But keep an open mind. Once I got past the first impression I realized that this is a place where thousands of eager young hands explore and learn in the best possible way—by doing.

Consider the everyday action of breaking an egg. You're probably thinking: whack the thing on the side of a bowl. Not at the science centre. Here, when groups of youngsters tackle the problem, it's a full-scale engineering project involving the dynamics of pulleys, ramps and levers. Some take the Humpty Dumpty approach, where the egg moves to its destruction. Others favour the Willie Coyote method, designing their machine to strike the egg. Either way, the Rube Goldberg contraptions they concoct, with everything from bricks to roller skates, get the job done. Scrambled eggs—unscrambled brains.

Experiments with static electricity often start with a simple balloon, but everyone wants to get in on the fun with the Van de Graff Generator. It's a hair-raising experience when science guy Kevin Aschenmeier instructs curious kids (and willing-to-try-anything-for-a-story writers) to take hold of the electrifying metal globe. You can tell he's having as much fun as we are.

Other stations offer do-it-yourself learning, but Kevin's there if you want some help or more in-depth info. He'll tell you about the monks and the Tower of Hanoi and get you thinking about optical illusions

At a Glance

and infinity with the mirror triangle. Play with Newton's Cradle or ride the gyro chair. And if you're trying to get your kids (or your spouse—I'm definitely thinking of taking Bruce to this place) to appreciate the value of electricity, have a go at cranking the handle and find out just how much energy it takes to light a single bulb. Check out the air quality monitoring station and get a graphic look at the pollution we breathe. The climate change exhibit is a great source for tips on doing your bit to save energy and help the environment.

When the kids have had enough earth-bound reality, take the stairway to the stars for a look through the Space for Space gallery, then plant your butt on the floor in the mini planetarium. In the blacked-out dome, I lose all sense of perspective as the heavenly bodies cross the night sky and Kevin tells the Greek, Egyptian, Viking and North American Native stories of the constellations along with an array of scientific facts.

The science centre lays on a whole range of programs for individuals and groups. As well as the self-guided tour and planetarium experience, it brings in travelling exhibits like Dinosaurs Unearthed, Bugs and Beyond and Sky Hunters. Every Saturday afternoon the learning includes creative projects the kids (of any age) can take home. There's science for preschoolers, science camp for school breaks and science themed birthday parties.

I strike up a conversation with a couple of boys in the main gallery. "We try to get here every week," says Kris, who tells me he's thirteen. When his ten-year-old brother Ben chimes in, I can't keep track of who's talking. "It's fun to build robots—get hands-on—get to think—no boundaries—no rules—get to see how things work . . ." How much better is that than the Xbox.

Davison Orchards Pumpkin Festival

ALEX ISN'T SURE WHAT IT'S ALL ABOUT when we announce our trip to Davison Orchards. At two-and-a-half, his experience with farms is all but non-existent. Being a typical city kid, I'm sure it never crossed his busy little brain that the food on his plate came from anywhere but the supermarket where he loves to ride the kiddy-car shopping cart. Imagine his joy when he learns that this place has its own special ride—although it takes a while to make the discovery with so much fun stuff between the parking lot and the Johnny Popper tour.

The sun holds the promise of heat later in the day, but the bright autumn morning is still crisp and clear with tufts of white cloud in an Okanagan blue sky backing Davison's brightly painted Country Village, a heavy load of red apples on the trees and crowds of jack-o'-lanterns-in-waiting in the pumpkin patch.

The moment we're away from the parking lot, Alex is in toddler heaven. No need to keep a grip on the little guy's hand when he spots the playground and races for his turn to shoot out of the mini red barn's hayloft on an irresistible big yellow slide. His mom and grandpa and I drop onto a bench under a massive spreading shade tree and let him work off the car ride from Kelowna.

Something overhead catches my attention and I look up to see a guy in blue coveralls shinnying out the branch to rescue a stranded kitten. Did I mention the kitten is plush and stuffed—oh yeah—and the rescuer has a pumpkin head. We meet lots more of these veg-heads as we walk around the farm—a pumpkin man riding his bicycle across the lawn, a pumpkin-person band twanging out country and western tunes

At a Glance

Davison Orchards is open daily May through October. Plan on a couple of hours (especially with kids in tow) to check out the orchards, Critter Coral, playground, Country Village and take a ride on the Johhny Popper apple box tractor ride. Davison Orchards is five minutes east of downtown Vernon. Take 30th Avenue, which turns into Bella Vista Road, to Davison Road. See map on page 117. For more info and details on special events, visit www.davisonorchards.ca.

Alex picks his first pumpkin at Davison Orchards, Vernon.

and a big pumpkin farmer all dressed up for family pics.

When Alex has ploughed a couple of fields on the playground tractor and slid about a thousand times out of the hayloft, we judge it's time to move on and I manage to coax him away with the promise of a ride behind a real tractor. He's reluctant—after all, what can be better than the red barn slide—but since Grandma's offering, he agrees. (Grandma's are magic.)

We join the line for the Johnny Popper pumpkin patch ride and are soon bumping along through an orchard laden with fruit and heavy with the smell of ripe apples. Alex is predictably thrilled to be riding in an apple box behind a big John Deere. Easy for him, the kid's only three feet tall. But picture an apple box, you know the red crates you see piled up around orchards all over the valley in autumn, now picture that apple box crammed with one kid and three substantial adults. You're grinning. (About now I'm thinking his dad is lucky he had to work today.)

The big green tractor pulls our little red train up the hillside and around the rim of a dusty field that looks like a kindergarten art project where the kids were given only orange paint. Hundreds of pumpkins dot the ground. We pull to a stop and the race is on. Kids and big kids jump down from the crates and fan out like special forces in search of the perfect jack-o'-lantern.

Grandpa Bruce takes command of our foraging party. He leads Alex to a cluster of likely candidates and begins the boy's education. Not too big, nice and round, no serious blemishes, good hollow sound when you rap on the shell. Alex listens to every word then makes straight for a lopsided, rough-skinned monster big enough to make it as Cinderella's coach. Happily he can't budge the thing and Bruce is able to edge him toward just the right specimen. Alex hefts his prize and insists on carrying it back to the train, "by myself."

He cradles the pumpkin on his lap as we return through the orchard, among the rows of trees, tall and small, labelled Spartan, Yellow Delicious, Gala and Macintosh. We trundled past a fenced enclosure and I point out the sheep and goats. That does it. Alex can hardly wait for the train to stop. He shoves the pumpkin at his mother, grabs my hand and heads for the other kids (couldn't resist).

When we get to the Critter Coral, he stops for a minute to take it

Pumpkin kids up to mischief on the bakery roof at Davison Orchards, Vernon.

all in—a contented looking ewe lying on her haunches munching her lunch, a trio of raucous goats shouldering each other out of the way to get the snack a youngster is holding through the fence, an old Billy marching across the goat bridge overhead—but what really snags his attention is a pulley contraption that raises a tin of food pellets to the top of the bridge.

Alex immediately grasps the concept. I buy pellets from a dispenser and he loads the tin, then cranks the handle and watches it rise on the pulley to the top where Billie nosed out his treats. We'd still be there if a little girl all dressed in pink hadn't come along looking for a turn. The complete gentleman (and budding lady's man), Alex relinquishes his spot and moves over to where he can feed the ground-level goats.

I pour a few pellets into his hand and he thrusts it through the fence to the impatient animal. Alex grins and giggles at the feel of the soft tongue on his palm and scampers from one pen to another feeding goats and sheep and even a patient donkey until I run out of quarters for the feed machine. Eventually, I lure him away with the promise of a snack for us.

We've lost track of the others, so back in the village, we climb up inside the silo tower, stopping to check out the historic farm photos on display, and from the window at the top easily spotted Mom and Grandpa sitting on a bench munching caramel apples and it looks like they've got a couple of spares. Hasty descent.

While we were feeding the farm critters, they'd looked after feeding us. Along with what appears to be the market's entire inventory of deep dish apple pies (bliss), the load of booty includes apple juice, apple butter and in a token nod to healthy farm-fresh eating, a bag of crisp, ripe apples. I'm ashamed to admit that as I eat my caramel apple, I can't take the pervasive aroma of cinnamon any longer and buy half a dozen apple cider donuts for the road. Love that farm-fresh food.

Pumpkin characters hang out all over Davison Orchards in October.

Geocaching

GEO-WHAT? Think high-tech hide-and-seek ... think new-age treasure hunt.

Geocaching is a game/hobby/obsession with a mushrooming world-wide following, including (predictably) my dad, the octogenarian mountain goat who loves precise techie-instruments almost as much as bushwhacking. He was mapping his tracks with a handheld GPS before most hikers had even heard of the technology (years before units in our cars started giving directions to the pizzeria). Anyway, put the two together and you've got a man in heaven. Naturally, he ropes me in.

The challenge starts on the Internet at www.geocaching.com where you search by postal code or country to find a list of caches in a particular area. My latest search has pulled up five hundred and seventeen sites within forty kilometres of my house in the Central Okanagan. Since the first cache was hidden in Oregon on May 2, 2000, well over a million caches have been placed in over two hundred countries with more being added every day.

On the website, the summary page gives the techno-mountain goat enough information to help narrow the field (I let him pick the caches and just go along for the hike) and when he clicks on the caches that interest him, he gets an individual page with full details including coordinates, an overview map, the difficulty of both terrain and hiding place, sometimes a clue to help in the search, photos of the area and a log of the geocachers who have previously found it. In the early

At a Glance

A GPS receiver is essential. Options include dedicated units as well as GPS enabled mobile phones and PDAs. Prices for dedicated units, mostly made by Garmin and Magellan, start around $100 but can run to over three times as much if you load them up. No need for simple geocaching. I have a very basic and elderly model that does the job just fine. Do look for something sturdy, small and waterproof with the best battery life you can find. Take time to get used to your GPS before heading into the field. For an online tutorial visit www.trimble.com/gps. For information on caches go to www.geocaching.com.

days, he would print the page or just write down the coordinates, but all things technological keep advancing and now he can download all the data into his GPS to coordinate with its onboard maps—wizard!

On my first expedition, he let's me off easy with a cache rated two stars out of five on both the difficulty and terrain scales. The starting point is at a recreation centre parking lot and I soon realize the GPS is directing us down a well-worn trail. It's a typical Okanagan morning, dry and sunny with the temperature steadily climbing. We walk through a stand of red-barked ponderosa pines with the scent of wild roses in the air. At the first waypoint we change direction and walk down a moderate hillside covered in roses and Saskatoon bushes.

When the GPS says we've found ground zero, the real treasure hunt begins. Caches come in many shapes and sizes and there's a whole variety of different types. You might find something as small as a film canister containing a message, hidden in the crook of a tree, or a sturdy plastic container buried under the cover of branches and leaves, or an historic plaque or monument. You have to be alert, literally searching high and low. From frustrating experience, I can testify that finding the right coordinates by no means guarantees finding the cache.

But this time, zigzagging back and forth in a small search grid we get lucky within a few minutes, spotting the container—a green metal can with a spring-lock lid—under a Saskatoon bush camouflaged by dry branches. Yee-haw! It may sound crazy, but we're totally buzzed to get the cache open and find the treasure inside. Traditional caches usually contain a surprise. The treasure might be a hat or book or a toy, whatever the last person left behind. That's the etiquette—when you find a cache, if you take the treasure, you leave something else for the next person. Later, when you log your find on the website, you include a note about what you took and what you left.

This cache is a bonanza. Among the goodies inside—a keychain, rubber airplane, small jewel box—we discover a Bart Simpson figure wearing what looks like a military dog tag. It's a travel bug.

Travel bugs are really valuable for parents who want their kids to learn some geography. When you take a bug from a cache, you don't keep it, you move it on. Each transfer is recorded on the website, so the person or family who originally placed it can follow their bug's journey

Dad and I check out a geocache on Knox Mountain in Kelowna.

and travel online. The timing is great for me because I'm on my way to Toronto, so Bart the travel bug gets his first plane ride and I snap his pic next to the CN Tower to post online. Some travel bugs have made it all the way around the world. On that same trip, Bruce and I try geocaching on our own and uncover a cache in the wilds of High Park.

With geocaching, you decide where you want to look and how demanding you want the exercise to be. Dad usually opts for something involving a backcountry trek, but I also know a couple that only goes after caches that are easy to reach from the highway. They pre-map a selection of sites before taking off on trips in their RV. Heather, a geocacher who once worked in forestry but now deals with teens at risk and kids in school break child care programs, says it's the best scam ever for prying kids away from their Xboxes and out into the (shudder!) fresh air. When Dad introduced the idea to my nephews on a visit to Ontario, they got so hooked, they commandeered their parents' Blackberries to play. My grandson Alex can't read the GPS yet, but when Grandma gets on those hiking boots, he's game to go along for the treasure hunt.

CrocTalk

ALLIGATORS AND CAIMANS, turtles and tortoises, even two endangered African cats—now we're talking. Most of the animals Doug Illman shelters at his crocodilian education centre, CrocTalk, are rescues from unsuitable environments, often the result of people buying exotic pets, then being unable to care for them. Doug, whose childhood interest in dinosaurs expanded into a passion for crocodilians, has made it his life's work to rescue animals, inform people and change attitudes.

A skilled mural painter with close to five hundred works in local homes, restaurants, bars and public spaces (proceeds help to fund CrocTalk), Doug has created a tropical setting for the live croc species and his supercroc dino display with a separate desert backdrop for the cats.

I have to admit that Carlos, the African Caracal, and Cleo, the African Serval, appeal most to me —I'm more of a cat woman than a gator gal. Cleo, in particular, takes a real shine to me. Doug and his partner Brenda are knocked out when she sniffs at my hand, climbs her front paws up my leg and lets me pet her. But I digress.

The reptilian attractions are definitely interesting, even if not quite so close to my heart. I fall in love with Sheridan the tortoise, who contrary to his species' reputation, moves so fast I have trouble getting a shot of him. The kids around me go wild (and I step back a pace) when Doug hefts Alli McGator in his arms. We're talking fair-sized critter—serious teeth—and she just smiles (well, it looks like a smile, like I said, lots of teeth. Check out my photo of this little drama on the CrocTalk homepage). Of course, most of the kids want to hold one too. Fortunately, Doug has some junior-sized crocs (or caimans—darned if I can tell them apart—guess I should have listened more closely) for them to touch.

At a Glance

CrocTalk is a conservation and education facility focused on crocodilians and endangered wildcats located at 4493A Stewart Road East, in Kelowna. For details on birthday parties, special events, hours and directions, visit www.croctalk.com.

Alli's pals Lucky McGator and Lucy McGator are also impressive. Lucy is another of Doug's rescues. She spent seven years with the UBC zoology department and was headed for the big sleep when he stepped in and found a way to build another enclosure and fit her into a new retirement home. These guys have it pretty good. Each of the pools has in-floor heating to keep the temperature suitably tropical and Doug and Brenda are fanatical about hygiene. The pools are emptied and cleaned with all natural products every three days.

Something must be working right, because a couple of the caimans have been making whoopie. Doug has an incubator filled with sixteen eggs. He'll keep some of the hatchlings and the rest will be released in protected wildlife refuges.

Conservation through education is Doug's mantra. He says, "To change the future, we've got to change the minds of our kids." But he's expanded his definition of kids. Apparently adults are often the ones who don't want to leave. I get that.

Doug Illman cuddles Alli McGator at his CrocTalk conservation and education facility in Kelowna.

I relate better to Carlos the African Caracal.

Osoyoos Desert Model Railway

WHEN A MODEL TRAIN OBSESSION runs completely amok and sucks in a whole family like an Oklahoma tornado in full twist, you wind up with the Osoyoos Desert Model Railway. If the trains (and buses and cars) weren't moving, you'd hardly notice the track system that anchors a fantasy of mini mountain villages, ski resorts, farms and cityscapes. Poul Pedersen (the obsessed) says there's no master plan. He just lays down the tracks and his wife Ulla and daughter Lottie create a Lilliputian world around them. Sorry, I'm mixing literary images here—I could throw in Tom Thumb for good measure. You see where I'm going with this.

The Pedersen's wee world is populated by even weer figures, something over nine thousand of them (it's so easy to lose track) that are actually about half the size of Thumbelina, and by some miracle of manual dexterity, Ulla hand-paints each one. I'm boggled by the minuscule faces with carefully applied eyes the size of a pin head and Thumbelina could have blown me over when I learned that Ulla actually started working on the models as therapy for severe rheumatic arthritis. In all, she's assembled more than eighteen hundred models and painted over eighteen thousand little figures (people from all over want to buy them).

The layout fills a thirty-five hundred square foot space, but you have to get in close to appreciate the humour and applied story-telling ability of this family team. I'll give you a few hints—look for the scuba diver and mermaid, the police making an arrest and four weddings and a funeral. You can play Where's Waldo all day, unless you're just hypnotized by the trains.

At a Glance

Osoyoos Desert Model Railway is open year round. It's located in a bit of an out-of-the way place in a light industrial zone, but isn't too tough to find. Get all the tiny details at www.osoyoosrailroad.com.

Above and facing page: Paragliders soar over the valley near Lumby.

Chapter 11

Off Beat

FACE IT, I NEEDED A CATCH-ALL, a place to put some of
my quirky experiences and Okanagan oddities that just wouldn't
pigeon-hole neatly into the other eleven chapters. So here it is,
everything from jumping off a mountain to tracking killer mushrooms,
searching the outback for lost mines to searching the waters of
Okanagan Lake for illusive monsters. One thing I've learned about
life in this valley, if it's dull, you're just not looking hard enough.

Paragliding

I DON'T FEEL A BIT NERVOUS (she says), and it's true—not that I can say the same about other members of my family. For some reason, they're less than enthusiastic about my determination to jump off a mountain. You'd think they'd be thrilled.

Veteran paraglider and instructor Glenn Derouin negotiates the switchbacks on the dry forest service road, climbing through the rangeland on the flank of Vernon Mountain to the launch site. Doug Mitchie, another instructor with Paraglide Canada is along to return the vehicle to the landing zone. Glenn's pooch Auber (short for slobber—and I can vouch for the reason) sits with his head between the seats, panting. Glenn says he'll be really disappointed when he realizes he's not going to fly.

Nearly invisible in the dust cloud behind, Bruce gamely brings up the rear in our four-by-four. He's accepted the assignment of documenting my flight for posterity (and possible insurance claims should the family's misgivings prove founded).

No doubt hoping to allay fears that I don't actually feel, Glenn fills me in on the sport and what to expect on our tandem flight. The wing is made of ripstop nylon, the lines are Kevlar with a polyester sheath and we'll be packing a parachute. He points to the surrounding ridges, indicating the fluffy white mass of gathering cumulus clouds. That's what we're after. These clouds grow on the thermals that will keep us aloft. "Just nice," he says, adding that what we have to watch out for is "overdeveloping cloud"—the kind of pillar formation that gets taller than it is wide.

At a Glance

The North Okanagan is prime paragliding country with some of the best terrain and most consistent weather conditions in Western Canada. Glenn Derouin learned to paraglide in France during the early years of the sport. He's been teaching since 1989 and for over a decade has operated Paraglide Canada in Vernon. For details on tandem flights and lessons, visit www.paraglidecanada.com.

"We want to keep our distance from those," he says. "Around ODs you can get caught in the strong updrafts and before you know it you're at twenty to thirty thousand feet (where you freeze or pass out from lack of oxygen)."

I begin to see why Glenn calls paragliding "a thinking man's sport. You have to control your fear. You're always thinking, plan A—B—C. You're always looking and calculating the air…. It's better to be on the ground wishing you were in the air than being in the air wishing you were on the ground." I get that.

Pilots have to learn aerodynamics and meteorology as well as flying skills. Glenn trots out another catchy instructor-type phrase to underscore the point. "You want to use superior knowledge to avoid using superior skills."

In this context it's less of a surprise to learn that the average age of pilots is in the forty-five to fifty range. "It's people who are a little older," he says, "maybe their knees are gone, whatever, but they still want a thrill sport."

And I'm about to find out for myself. Doug hops out to open a cattle gate and we park in the meadow beyond. We're jumping from Baldy Launch, a site that was originally used by hang gliders. There's a steep little climb to the top of the barren hump and Glenn is puffing a little under the weight of the twenty-three-kilogram tandem pack. (The single flyer version weighs about half as much.) Okay, so I'm puffing too, even though I'm only toting a couple of cameras—definitely not nerves.

Doug helps Glenn spread the wing on the ground, carefully checking to make sure all of the lines are straight and untangled. Auber dances around the perimeter. He's ready to fly—poor guy.

When the gear is in position, Glenn takes me through the takeoff procedure, explaining slowly and clearly. I listen very carefully. My mouth is a little dry as I repeat the instructions aloud. There's a drum solo in my rib cage and my palms are just slightly damp when I grasp the harness. The sling I'll ride hangs loose. Glenn takes his position behind me.

Bruce has disappeared below the lip of the hill, already in position to record the fateful leap. Doug nabs Auber (who I fancy gives me a venomous look) but suddenly there's nothing in my consciousness but the sound of Glenn's commands and the feel of the wind.

"One, two, three …" I take a deep breath. "Step, step."

That little forward motion is enough to lift the edge of the wing into the air and although Glenn had warned me, I almost lose my balance at the instant yank.

"Walk, walk, walk," he commands.

I lean into the harness like a draught horse pulling a heavy plough, astonished at the weight of the sail trying to drag us backward. Then I sense the lift as the sail starts to rise.

"Run, run, run."

The command is urgent in my ear—and that's it. We're airborne. I remember to feed my arms through the straps, grab the toggles and slide my butt onto the seat.

Floating, we're floating, with only the gentle sound of the wind to mark our passage. I want to scream with the sheer delight of it. But I hold my tongue, unwilling to spoil the peace of the moment. Below, the mountainside falls away and I see scattered cattle on the still spring-green grasslands and among the firs and pines. Glenn says gliders often see deer and moose and even bears from the air. The animals, accustomed to looking left and right for intruders and with no sound to give away the approaching wing, aren't frightened off.

We drift downward, past the windsock at King Eddy, a lower launch site and I begin to fear that the ride would soon be over. I spot an eagle winging by and think, wow, that's a big bird. But Glenn's reaction is different. "Let's follow him," he says. Immediately the wing tilts and I'm looking virtually straight down as we bank. Then we catch the thermal and my stomach stays behind in the sudden lift.

"Yippee!" This time I can't contain it. We ride the warm updraft in tight circles climbing with the eagle, higher and higher until we're far above Baldy Launch.

Now I understood how pilots manage to stay aloft for long flights. Glenn says the Canadian record is two hundred and fifty-six kilometres, while the world record is an astonishing four hundred and sixty. He says it's easy to do fifty to seventy kilometres here and he regularly makes three-hour flights from Vernon to Salmon Arm or Sicamous, climbing to the cloud base at 2,400 to 3,000 metres. Golden is another popular target.

"You like that," Glenn asks. Not bothering to wait for the obvious answer he whips us into a wing over. "Let's pull some Gs," he shouts and we nose down into a spiral dive then catch the thermal and climb again. I'd gladly stay up here all day, hanging out with the birds. Not that I feel moved to want to take up the sport on my own, but flying tandem with a competent pilot is awesome.

Eventually Glenn has to take aim for the landing zone and he gives me instructions. Bum to the edge of the seat, feet forward. (There goes my heart again.) That ground is coming up mighty fast. I execute a gentle skid and stop on my backside (supposed to stay on my feet—oops). Glenn manages not to topple over me. We unbuckle and set to carefully folding the wing. There's no sign of the others, which is a little disappointing, because there won't be any photos of the landing—well, maybe that isn't such a bad thing.

The equipment is all packed away when a moving dust cloud announces their arrival (engine trouble on the way down). Auber's exuberant tail wag indicates that all is forgiven. We shake paw to hand and head off. On the way home, I realize that I'm looking at the clouds differently. That thin pillar rising out of the fluffy cumulus has definitely ODed. But not me, I'm totally ready for more.

I grab a self-snap as pilot Glenn Derouin chases the eagles on our tandem paraglide flight east of Vernon.

Mascot Mine

FLYSPECK ON THE BC ROADMAP, Hedley once boasted hotel bars open 24-7 (the better to serve off-duty miners) and four or five brothels (ditto). Large-scale gold mining started early in the 20th century, the *Gazette* began printing the news and the Similkameen Valley's first bank opened its teller cage. But the new millennium dawned on a sleepy little backwater that had gradually descended to near oblivion after the mines closed and most traffic between the Okanagan and the Coast abandoned Highway 3 for another route.

That Hedley suddenly stands on the brink of a second gold rush is due to a quirky twist of fate involving the Upper Similkameen Indian Band and a played out mine. I pick up the story at a foursquare ochre-red building in the middle of town. The former schoolhouse (1939 to 2004), reborn as the Snaza'ist Discovery Centre, is home base for a unique attraction, the Mascot Gold Mine Tour.

Browsing the centre's airy exhibition rooms I learn that the Similkameen people have mined the striated rock faces in the area they call, Snaza'ist (that's *sna-za-ee-st*) meaning striped rock place, for thousands of years. You have to see the surrounding cliffs to fully appreciate their gravity-defying skills—extracting ochre for paint, chert for arrowheads and products like opals, quartz crystals and even gold for trade and personal use.

The 19th century was half over before white prospectors turned up—even then in only a trickle, nothing like the rushes that surged into the Fraser Valley, the Cariboo and the Yukon. And while some struck it

At a Glance

The town of Hedley is located about a one-hour drive west of the Okanagan Valley on Hwy 3. The Snaza'ist Discovery Centre is open daily from late May to mid-October for self-guided tours and a guided archeology program. Mascot Gold Mine tours also operate daily from late May through mid-October. Budget at least half a day for the two attractions and dress in layers for the cooler temperatures in the mine. The mine tour is not suitable for people with mobility restrictions or health issues. For details visit www.mascotmine.com.

Vintage ore car waits at the loading chute in the Mascot Mine, Hedley.

Viewpoint at Mascot Mine overlooks the village of Hedley over nine hundred metres below.

rich panning the creeks, the first hard rock mine didn't open until 1904, launching Hedley's short-lived golden age. Earth-toned interpretive displays, echoing the colours of the striped rocks, and a stunningly surreal Vancouver-produced video make the connection with the Mascot.

In 1899, a hard-luck prospector named Duncan Woods identified a sixteen hectare unclaimed sliver of Nickel Plate Mountain and staked it as the Mascot Fraction. Trouble erupted five years later when the adjoining Nickel Plate Mine found it's main ore body angled into the Fraction and superintendent Gomer P. Jones met Woods to suggest a deal. Nobody knows just what happened, but the ensuing feud lasted until Woods finally sold his claim to the Vancouver-based Hedley

Mascot Gold Co. in 1933. The wily old prospector, who by this time was close to eighty, grumbled: "I got all this money, now what can I do with it?"

The new company had its own problems. That old nemesis, the Nickel Plate, owned the other side of the mountain leaving the Mascot nothing but a sheer cliff access—over nine hundred metres above town. Working from a string of buildings perched on tiny footholds in the all-but-vertical rock face, miners had to tunnel almost a kilometre to reach the ore body. Then the only way to get the ore to the smelter in town, and the easiest way to transport both men and supplies, was a Hail Mary! ride on the Mascot's aerial tram.

These are the features that make the Mascot such a unique part of our provincial heritage—a bit of heritage that was nearly lost.

Aboard the tour bus on the forty-five minute ride to the mine site, tour guide Harry Alton, an outdoorsy looking guy wearing a prospector's beard and a feather-accented Indiana Jones hat, fills in the story. After operations ended in 1949, the buildings lay abandoned, slowly decaying for more than fifty years. Eventually they were slated to share the fate of other historic BC mining structures like Hedley's own smelter—purposely burned to the ground.

For a time the Mascot was reprieved with a provincial heritage site designation. But when funding was withdrawn in the mid-90s, the mine again faced doom. Enter the Upper Similkameen Indian Band. Recognizing the tourism potential (that apparently escaped government officials), the Band bought the mine and (heavy on the irony here) rescued an important remnant of white history. Restoration has been ongoing since 1995. Now with the creation of the Snaza'ist Centre and the Mascot Gold Mine Tour, the whole town's future looks brighter.

Shannon Beglaw expertly manoeuvres our bus around forty-eight switchbacks as we climb to 1,620 metres on a gravel road smooth enough that I can decipher my notes without too much guesswork. She adds short sidebars to Harry's commentary—"mostly fir and lodgepole pine with more aspens as we get higher up…the Indian paint brush is red and those yellow daisy-like things are brown-eyed Susans….See the piles of rocks and logs in that dried up tailing pond—they were put there specially for the marmots….Keep an eye peeled through this stand of aspens, we've been seeing a doe with two fawns in here the last week."

We don't see mama deer among the trees—she's browsing at the edge of a meadow a half-kilometre farther on.

The bus ride ends at a narrow turnaround wedged between the rocky tree line and—space. We shoulder into our jackets (it's cooler up here) and follow Harry along a contour-hugging track. He stops before an unpromising tangle of sagging timbers hanging over emptiness and a massive red and white sign that reads: Danger Keep Out. Surely this isn't the Mascot. Harry cracks a grin that says: I love this part, and launches into his spiel.

The Canty and Good Hope mines, too small to support their own mills, trucked their ore here and loaded it onto an aerial tram for transport to the Mascot. Interesting—but the best part of this stop is the view. There's an alpine feel to the distant snow-spangled rim of Cathedral Ridge and far below, the green-edged Similkameen River threads through the valley past the Tinker-toy village of Hedley.

Down the track we round a rocky outcrop and do a Keystone Cops routine when Harry stops short. A young mountain goat regards us with mild surprise, briefly considers, then skittles down the loose talus bank, a chorus of shutters ba-zeeping in his wake. We have to follow him down the giddy slope, but our route is a series of sturdy wooden stairways that jig and jag toward a clutch of shiny tin roofs about a million miles below.

"Six hundred steps going down—seven hundred coming up!"

This from a man who knows what he's talking about. Mike Lich, our second guide, worked on the reconstruction, regularly navigating these stairs with an armload of two-by-fours balanced on his shoulder.

By comparison, our descent is easy. We stop at the cookhouse level where a spur-line from the tram dropped supplies right on the cook's doorstep. Down another flight is the main level and mine entrance. Harry and Mike kit us up with white hard hats and headlamps powered by a battery pack (heavy) that straps around your waist. One behind the other we file through the granite portal. Our lights cast triangular beams that bob in random patterns along the damp curved walls.

"This is the ventilation pipe," says Harry. His words bounce off the stone, landing in my ears from many directions. He explains that, for

Mascot Mine buildings cling to the side of Nickel Plate Mountain, Hedley.

Surreal moment in the Mascot Mine, Hedley.

safety, the pipe is always strung on the left side as you enter a mine. That way, if the lights should fail, you can always find your way out by feeling for the pipe and keeping it on your right. To make the point, he instructs us to turn off our headlamps. Complete—utter—impenetrable blackness. (Note to self—pipe on right!)

To lighten the mood Harry challenges us to name the Seven Dwarfs—we come up with five—and whistling *Off to Work We Go*, marches us deeper into the mine. At a junction of two tunnels he groups us along the wall and suddenly we're in the midst of a work crew—shovelling ore, filling skips, preparing to blast. The sound and light show is incredible.

Back in the sunshine we have plenty of time to poke around and check out the displays in the former compressor room. A scale model of the mine and underground workings is all the more remarkable when you consider what must have been involved in getting it here.

Life on the cliff had its compensations: $4.75 a day (good money in 1941); card games in the cook house; and three squares whipped up by cooks so good the miners from the Nickel Plate often hiked over for pie. Safety dictated a strict no-whisky rule, though some miners obviously didn't get the memo as restoration crews found numerous empties in the building walls.

On a lookout ramp, I'm joined by a canyon wren that doesn't know the *Hi Ho* song but has a pretty good tune of his own. I'm glad to take it easy for a few minutes before the inevitable. Climbing back to the landing doesn't prove too bad, although a seven-year-old in the group sparks considerable envy when she scoots by us—a pink streak *running* up the steps.

We're breathing normally by the time Shannon appears with the next group and we load up the bus for the return trip. Part way down (after spotting two bucks browsing on a hillside) she stops at a lookout for photos and brake check. Under the trees I notice a trio of mauve flowers and start shooting—the mariposa lilies are in bloom.

With an all-around experience like this—great cultural centre, underground mine show and an alpine eco-adventure—Hedley's future is looking golden.

Touring the Mascot
Mine in Hedley.

Mushroom Mania

EIGHT OF US CIRCLE AROUND naturalist Roseanne Van Ee in the parking lot of the Vernon Visitors Centre. She reads a passage from one of her heavily thumbed field guides, this one by David Arora. "All that the rain promises ... the miracle of mushrooms in their spontaneity ..." It's her way of launching the tour and underlining how lucky we are after days of poor weather to be setting out on a crisp, mid-October morning to hunt for mushrooms. We pile into the van with her associate Reg at the wheel and head east on Highway 6 for Lumby and the turn north to Mabel Lake.

Driving through the valley past the Coldstream Ranch, someone asks one of those "I wonder" questions about cattle. Roseanne answers, "I'm more of an expert on bats and bears"—and follows up with a tutorial. That's what it's like on her tours. The former national and provincial park naturalist has spent decades padding her knowledge of Okanagan flora and fauna. If she doesn't know an answer off the top of her head (and that doesn't happen very often), she'll soon find it in one of her guides.

The talk turns from winged night prowlers (sixteen bat species in Canada, fourteen of them found in the Okanagan, according to Roseanne) to mushrooms—magical, munchable and deadly. She tells us that commercial harvesters come to this region to scoop up morels, chanterelles, oyster mushrooms and pine mushrooms (traditionally roasted, she adds, unable to resist an aside, but also barbecued and baked ... never fried!)

At a Glance

Autumn in the Okanagan produces a brilliant display of funky fungi. But unless you really know what you're doing (or want to play Russian roulette with your dinner), don't go mushrooming on your own. Roseanne Van Ee offers guided tours to the Mabel Lake area in October. These are intended as educational outings. You'll get a few mushrooms to take home, but collecting isn't the primary objective. Bring your camera. For details visit www.outdoordiscoveries.com.

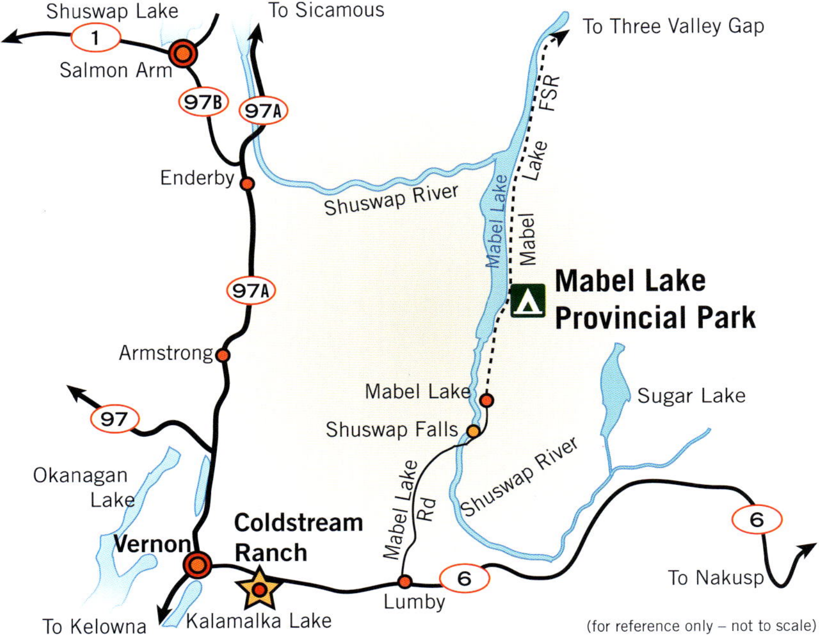

She continues with the information that morels are more common in spring, although you may find them in autumn. But then you have to be very careful. "Every edible mushroom has a look-alike," she says. "Mildly or very poisonous." (I'm starting to pine for a good cello-wrapped portobello from the green grocer.)

Beyond Lumby we roll through pastures carved in blocks from the forest. Horses, brown cows and, living in individual pup-tent-style wooden hutches, what must be the world's happiest pigs. Backlit amber-leafed aspens, windrow poplars, cottonwoods and a stand of reforested larch warm the landscape. On the Mabel Lake Forest Service Road we cross the Shuswap River and pass the BC Hydro dam that creates Shuswap Falls.

"Look for eagles and herons," says Roseanne, "maybe a bear in the off-channel oxbows—oh, there's a deer."

The pavement gives way to gravel and a bald eagle paces us for a half-kilometre, floating just above the hydro lines.

"Shaggy manes on the left!"

Reg hits the brakes and we pile out for a better look at the two-inch, hippy-haired domes clustered in the gravel. "They're really good with anything—with cream and pepper, great in Alfredo sauce or mushroom soup," says Roseanne, carefully cutting a specimen and dusting it off with a cloth. She explains that mushrooms shouldn't be washed (makes them mushy) and should be stored in open baskets or open paper bags—never plastic.

We're cautioned to cut the stems rather than rip them from the ground, which destroys the mycelia beneath. The part of the mushroom we see is just the fruiting body containing the spores of the fungus. The main growth is under the soil or bark or whatever medium they're found in. Only in perfect conditions, like after a rain, do the mushroom heads pop up.

Our safari begins in earnest at the Cascade Forest Service Trail after Roseanne lines us up for a group photo (while delivering a mini-lecture on the yew tree—not rare, but uncommon). Satisfied with the pic, she shoulders her backpack, assigns two of us to carry collection baskets—one for keepers we'll split up at the end of the day, one for

Roseanne points out footwear she contributed to the shoe tree at the entrance to Mystic Trail on Mabel Lake.

the scary killer guys—and heads into the forest.

The trail is a narrow wedge in the vertical bank of the canyon wall with exposed roots and slippery rocks to make the cushy, damp footing just a bit exciting.

"What's this…"

"Look at that…"

The group splinters and forages in the target rich environment then reforms as our guide flips open a Swiss Army knife and harvests a poisonous chanterelle—one for the do-not-eat basket.

We continue along the trail crouching to peer at a bright orange disk, a thimble-sized umbrella and countless LBMs (little brown mushrooms) adding more samples to the baskets. The sound of rush-

Without expert advice, I'll stick to photographing these tasty (or deadly) mushrooms.

Vegetarian seafood. Lobster mushrooms reputedly make a good substitute for the real thing.

ing water expands to a roar as we near the foot of Cascade Falls, a special bonus for me, the waterfall addict. But white water isn't our focus and after a brief photo op we head back to the van for the short hop to our next stop.

At Appele's Creek Roseanne introduces us to the Mabel Lake shoe tree (an eclectic assortment of footwear hung like ornaments on a roadside tree trunk), then leads us into a forest peopled with fantastic creatures and whimsical creations (Mystic Trail) until we suddenly emerge on a crescent beach, rimmed with fall colours and bathed in autumn sunshine. Lunch stop.

The day's last hunting ground is Mabel Lake Provincial Park. The one hundred and eighty-seven hectare preserve on the east shore of the lake (named for the daughter of a 19th century Hudson's Bay Company manager), features quite a different ecology than the dry grasslands and ponderosa parkland of the Okanagan.

This is a wetter zone where the Shuswap Highlands slope up to the Monashee Mountains creating the climate for cedar and hemlock forest. The park is popular with anglers who take rainbow trout from Taylor Creek (also a great place for spotting painted turtles) and often fish from the shores of the lake. In autumn, rainy days and cooler temps bring out the mushrooms.

Beneath a hemlock tree, Roseanne points out a truffle hole. Who knew? I thought these near mystical fungi were solely a southern European treasure, growing only around oak trees, rooted out by pigs and costing zillions. Not so. We have our very own. Smaller, humbler and much cheaper, but truffles nonetheless. And there are more luxury edibles on the forest floor—land-based lobster—big, lumpy, red mushrooms purported to be great with garlic and butter or cut into little pieces for seafood recipes.

The light is slanting low when Roseanne gathers us around a picnic table where we delve into her field guide library, trying to identify for ourselves the morsels in the baskets—especially the lethal ones— while she divvies up the spoils. Despite all we've learned, not for anything would I go mushrooming on my own, but I gladly accept one of Roseanne's precious paper goodie bags.

Ogopogo Spotting

IT'S TOUGH TO TAKE VERY SERIOUSLY a lake monster with a name like Ogopogo. But the creature of legend who's supposed to inhabit Okanagan Lake keeps resurfacing, at least in popular myth. And I'm willing to admit that odd riffles on the surface of the water give me pause—especially when I'm in it.

Some locals claim that Nessie, the Loch Ness Monster, and Ogopogo are one and the same. (Possibly after a dram or ten of Scotland's finest.) According to these wags, the creature migrates through a deep mid-earth waterway connecting Okanagan Lake and the Scottish loch. But most of us prefer to believe that Ogopogo is our very own. Called N'ha-a-itk (spelling varies) by the Okanagan People, her presence was first recorded several thousand years ago in stone pictographs that survive to this day.

Though the "devil of the lake" was once an object of fear, causing aboriginal people to sacrifice small animals to appease the demon before setting out in their canoes, our aquatic phantom has gradually gained a more benevolent persona.

Since European settlement in the mid-1800s, annual sightings have confirmed the general appearance of a large creature, some six or ten or maybe fifteen metres long, dark—possibly greenish in colour—with a narrow snake-like body usually seen as humps rising from the water about a metre-and-a-half apart. Ogopogo's head has been compared with a horse, a cow and even a goat with a beard. But all reports are consistent in their agreement that she moves with remarkable speed.

The name Ogopogo, derived from a 1920s music hall ditty, reflects the light-hearted affection with which we now view our elusive mascot. However, many outsiders take the search for her more seriously. Ogopogo hunts have been featured on the television programs *Unsolved Mysteries* and *Inside Edition*, and Japanese research teams have repeatedly combed the lake with divers and sophisticated underwater tracking equipment for their own televised documentaries. Google Ogopogo for a selection of amateur photos and videos.

Back in 2000/2001, the quest for our shy lake monster took a new twist when local businesses and Okanagan University College spon-

Close encounter with legendary Ogopogo on the Kelowna waterfront.

sored a $2 million reward for "indisputable evidence" of her existence. Of course, the proof had to be photographic, since Ogopogo is officially protected under British Columbia law. Remarkably, there was no payout.

But speculation continues. Folks in the know concentrate on the vicinity of an underwater cave near Peachland. Personally, I figure you're just as likely to spot Ogopogo from your beach blanket or Jet Ski as you are from a diving bell. So keep an eye out and your camera phone ready. Who knows, you might just scoop the world.

Above and facing page: Grapevines Restaurant at Gray Monk Estate Winery in Lake Country.

Chapter 12
Let's Eat

I LOVE FOOD. If you've read this far in the book, you've picked
up on the recurring theme. So it should come as no surprise that I
also love dining out. Cooking at home is fine—I actually enjoy it, a
lot—especially when Bruce and I get together in the kitchen with a
bottle of wine. But there are still loads of times when I just don't feel
like hauling out the pans and sharpening up the chef's knife. And
eating out gives me a chance to try other people's specialties. I'm
particularly partial to ethnic food—habit of a travel writer who's
eaten some of the best all over the world—and we have a surprisingly
wide selection of restaurants here in the Okanagan that serve up the
real thing from far away. We also have some very talented chefs who
work magic with our local products. I'd like to share every one of my
Okanagan dining delights with you, but I'm running out of pages. So
here's a selection representative of my eclectic tastes and presented
in regional order because I couldn't possibly pick favourites.

Brown Derby Café

3425 Pleasant Valley Road
Armstrong
250.546.8221

Owners Carolyn and Neil Todd don't have to say a word, their characters are stamped all over the place. A card on my table is very specific. "Listen carefully while your voluptuous and perky server titillates your taste buds with today's tantalizing treats." So when my voluptuous and perky server rushes up and reels off: "Mango, carrot and walnut soup; avocado, cream cheese, tomato and lettuce wrap or Reuben …" then stands with pencil poised over notepad, I'm all ears, but a little shaken (guessing the Brown Derby's mostly local trade already knows the regular line-up).

Apparently it dawns on Carolyn that my face doesn't look familiar, because she suddenly adds, "… or a menu …"—casts about and grabs one from an empty table. I go with the soup special (bright orange, sweet and yum!) and on the eavesdropped advice of a lady at the next table, a wedge of the pie for which "Carolyn wins ribbons at the fair."

For interest I check out the chatty breakfast menu. It warns: "Do not ask your server for basted or poached eggs—it won't happen." When I see items like the World Famous Egg Thing for $1.99 and the Not Quite so Famous Sausage Thing (but getting there!) for $2.50, I'm betting you have to share a table in the little dining room most mornings. The menu ends with an appeal: "Be nice to us—we are not morning people!" and I hear Neil singing along to the Beach Boys from the kitchen. What did I say about character?

Grapevine Restaurant

Gray Monk Estate Winery
1055 Camp Road, Okanagan Centre
250.766.3168

Gray Monk is one of the most venerable wineries in the Okanagan. In 1972, George and Trudy Heiss were among the first growers to get permission to make and sell wine from their own grapes, and their son George Jr. is carrying on the family tradition. The family pioneered adding food service to the winery experience and it's no surprise that they're also on the leading edge of wine touring.

We arrive for lunch at the onsite Grapevine Restaurant on a hot late-June afternoon, pretty much knackered from a morning's canoeing on Okanagan Lake. Nothing could be more welcome than a comfy chair under a beamy umbrella where I can contemplate the slope of the vineyard toward the blue water and the ridges beyond. Revived by a chilled, fruity Auxerrois, I'm soon tackling the menu created by Euro-trained chefs Willi Franz and René Haudenschild.

Several of my paddle-mates order wine flights (three different varietals to sample), others go with the menu's pairing suggestions. Soon fork duels erupt around the table (nothing to do with the wine) as we accept bites from each other's plates—hot smoked chicken salad (the special), veal sausage, almond crusted goat cheese with local greens, Fraser Valley duck confit, Qualicum scallops and tiger prawns, pulled pork melt…. There's no stopping us. When every crumb of the main course has disappeared we order more wine and switch to spoons. More cross-table tasting—crème brûlée with sun-dried cherries (sun-dried cherries! unbelievable) and fresh strawberries trimmed with frills of whipped cream.

The only problem with a meal at the Grapevine is that you can't really get away without stopping by the winery tasting room. So a few bottles of Pinot Gris and maybe a Latitude 50 or two just slide into the trunk…. Nothing to do with those flights at lunch. (Uh-huh.)

Little Tex

3302 29th Street, Vernon
250.558.5368

There are two dead giveaways for a good eatery. One: it's packed with locals at lunch. Two: the walls are papered in *Okanagan Life* magazine Best Restaurants Readers Choice Awards. Little Tex Café & Bistro in Vernon wins on both counts. Tucked away on a side street, this is a comfortable, modest little spot with a green and butternut colour scheme, tile floors, abstract paintings, saguaro cactus and steer skull wall art and a case of cultural confusion.

The menu lists thirteen burgers—from Thai to bison—and meals come with a choice of soup, Caesar, spinach or tossed salad, fries or combo. There's a daily soup special like Thai chorizo gumbo and after four, enchiladas, pizza and fajitas join the line-up. My portobello mushroom burger (no bun) was so amazing that I've added it to our home menu, although I can't quite match their chipotle mayo. Excellent.

Portobello mushroom burger (no bun) at Little Tex in Vernon.

Bouchons Bistro

1180 Sunset Drive, Kelowna
250.763.6595

In my Toronto corporate life back in the eighties, too many business dinners killed my desire for French food, but Bouchons has brought back the love. The place just feels right, instantly beaming me to another time and a little bistro in the Latin Quarter that still returns to my dreams. White linen, Dijon mustard walls, stained glass dividers and brass rails, dark wood, vintage globe light fixtures, the cabaret sounds of Ertha Kit and a cocktail menu with Kir Royale and Campari and soda.

Martine Lefèbvre, who alternates maître d ' duties with her husband Richard Toussaint (watching hockey tonight), is at the door to greet us looking chic and trim in an elegant skirt and sweater. (Women from Quebec always make me feel so dowdy, even when they don't have a background in the fashion industry like hers.) But she's so welcoming I forget my sartorial inferiority complex.

Bruce takes time with a wine list that deserves careful attention—more than one hundred and seventy labels specializing in Okanagan and French vintages and recognized by *Wine Spectator* as one of the most outstanding wine lists in the world. Our server, Marie-Claude, is one of the three staff sommeliers, so we put ourselves in her hands and concentrate on the food.

Dominique Couton's signature Chef's Table, essentially the daily special three-course meal with two selections for each course, appeals to Bruce while I go à la carte. His baked pear and blue cheese in flaky pastry tartlet starter is enough to make me like mouldy cheese. I attack fat escargots. Marie-Claude reminds me to let her know if I need more bread to soak up the garlic butter. I do.

My man tucks into duck breast on blackberry Merlot jus, I apply my Laguiole knife (can't miss the distinctive bee emblem) to rib steak with Syrah reduction, veggie medley and candied onions. We share the legendary paper cone of pommes frites presented in the centre of the table with mayo for dipping.

Marie-Claude slips in a little refresher, pepper-blackberry granular sorbet with fresh mint leaves that packs enough heat to make me peel down a layer (or was that a hot flash). My jacket is no more than half off when Martine zooms in to whisk it away.

Crème caramel with sliced kiwi, a strawberry and two blackberries reduces Bruce to a vacant stare and beatific smile. The perfect ending—but wait—Martine isn't done with us yet. One last little amuse-bouche, the chef's own black cherries preserved in vodka, kirsch and cognac. Enough said.

Servers ham it up at
Bouchons Bistro, Kelowna.

RauDZ (the restaurant formerly known as Fresco)

1560 Water Street, Kelowna
250.868.8805

Practically every woman spends some time in her life fanaticizing about the romantic moment when her special someone will pop the question. No, not the "what's for dinner tonight?" question, I'm talking about the "I think I've worked through my commitment issues and I'm hoping you'll take me on … for better or worse" question. Eyes misty, face alight, she nods—maybe even managing a weak "yes" as she lifts her left hand and begins an abiding love affair with that new ring.

Note to special someones: if you're going to fulfil that daydream, you've got to pick the right location. My fella made the perfect choice. His proposal (minus the commitment part) fit comfortably into the flow of a beautifully presented, professionally served and utterly delicious dinner at what was then the Okanagan's only four-diamond restaurant. Every meal at Fresco was an occasion made memorable by a team effort. The creations of chef Rod Butters and the others who worked their magic in the open kitchen were the foundation of this eatery's reputation. I won't soon forget the salad of fresh greens; the Carmeli's goat cheese tart; the venison sausage and elk; and the chef's signature beef that featured aged tenderloin and braised short rib, served that night with parsnips, tiny slender carrots, asparagus and beets.

But that wonderful food could so easily have been let down by mediocre service—something that wasn't about to happen with Audrey Surrao marshalling the front of house. It was no accident that our waiter knew just the right Okanagan wine, selected from Fresco's extensive cellar, to bring out the best in our food; that he chose exactly the right moment (right after I dabbed my eyes and before I started admiring my ring—again) to slip a pair of champagne-filled flutes onto the table and wish us joy; that he took note of how much I liked the candied walnuts accompanying the sliced apples on our cheese tray and brought me extras to enjoy with my port (unasked); or that he grinned with genuine pleasure when he presented a final dessert treat offering congratulations spelled out in drizzled chocolate (worthy of celebration all on its own).

Since that magical evening, Fresco has morphed into RauDZ. New hip look, new locally focused menu (with a couple of holdovers), same great service. I'm probably in the minority, missing the days of Fresco, but I do. Regardless, RauDZ is a cool spot.

RauDZ in Kelowna spotlights local producers.

Shady Rest British Fish & Chips

1359 Sutherland Avenue, Kelowna
250.860.2260

Nothing says comfort like fresh-cut fries and a chunk or two of flaky white fish encased in a steaming jacket of grease-oozing batter. In a nod to Canada's Food Guide you might toss in a side of slaw—although the creamy dressing probably puts it on the instantly-life-threatening-and-to-be-avoided-by-all-right-thinking-healthaholics list as well. But what the heck … (you're gonna love this rationalization). How can there be redemption without sin? If you can't defy the my-body-is-a-temple mantra once in a while, how are you to gain any sense of accomplishment, any feeling of moral superiority when you cosy up to a plate full of rabbit food? Surely you see the logic of my argument.

If you do (or you just love fish and chips—regardless), try this little den of iniquity on Kelowna's Sutherland Avenue. I mention the address, because, like all Okanagan newbies, I was astonished to learn that this morsel of an eatery—barely big enough for a clutch of stools and a single table—once occupied a space between Mill Creek and the highway to Vernon. Today, Sutherland is a leafy downtown residential street, a block south of Highway 97. But when it opened in 1946, the Shady Rest was a food stop on the main road, well out in the country, with dining space on the roof offering an uninterrupted view of the surrounding orchards.

Mel Pearson's dad bought the place in the 1960s and the family's been serving the same menu ever since. In Canada's Centennial year (1967), you could indulge your craving for two chunks of halibut and a mound of golden fries for just seventy cents (and nobody batted an eyelash at your food choice). For an extra dime, you could banish the summer heat by sliding an icy cold sugar and caffeine charged Pepsi between the metal rails to the bottle-sized opening in the bright yellow cooler. Prices have spiralled upward, but not much else has changed. The cooler still squats in the corner, takeout orders are still wrapped in newspaper and the air is still infused with the heart-warming (or stopping) scent of sizzling oil. Go ahead, sin a little.

A la Crêpe

Kelowna Farmers' and Crafters' Market
250.469.1915

Silvia Thomas calls them her little delights—les p'tits bonheurs de Silvia—but there's nothing little about the delight I take in her fruiti-licious crepes. I join the inevitable line-up and watch the tag-team show with Silvia and her partner, Helene Guy. Silvia, who hails from France's Loire Valley, cooks the crêpes, ladling a dollop of batter onto her round cooking surface, then at the moment of golden perfection, somehow manages to flip the platter sized wafer-thin pancakes with a wooden spatula. Off the grill to Helene for toppings and expert folding into an artful cone. When Helene says I can have it all—plus whipped cream … well.

Silvia Thomas wields her ladle and another golden crepe takes shape at A la Crêpe, Kelowna Farmers' and Crafters' Market.

Siam Orchid

279 Bernard Avenue, Kelowna
250.860.5600

Bit of advice—never cross a woman who can simultaneously juggle two sizzling woks, single-handedly cooking three-quarters of the food for a sixty-seat restaurant, while keeping an eye on a seriously cute toddler, Sebastian. Ron Yamada never does. Since he and Orathai opened the Siam Orchid, Ron's kept strictly to the front of house and left the kitchen to his mega-multi-tasking wife.

True, he does tag along on most of her annual Thai shopping trips—but don't get the wrong idea. Ron's not there to carry home bags of silk glad rags. Orathai's trips are all about food—the peppers, curries, lime leaves and Thai chillies that give her recipes the authentic flavour of her homeland. Let's be fair, though. While Ron downplays the importance of his role, legions of loyal regulars will tell you that his easy, customers-on-a-first-name style is just as important as the taste of Thailand that comes from Orathai's kitchen.

This guy is so accommodating that one very special Saturday afternoon he shut the restaurant down and hosted our wedding feast. When we arrived the tables were arranged in an open square that made for a wonderfully intimate gathering where we could see and easily talk to everyone. And when Alex, the ring-bearing grandson, was ready for a nap, we just bedded him down in a sleeping bag next to Sebastian in the makeshift nursery on the slightly raised platform where musicians play on weekends. It was perfect!

Don't expect to rush, this isn't fast food—remember the woman with the woks—she's making every dish to order ... mild, medium, hot, very hot and *Thai hot*! I can handle medium, but that's my limit, even after considerable practice and with a tongue-cooling pint of Tree Brewery's raspberry porter (outstanding with Thai food—I think it's even better than the traditional Singha).

Siam Orchid has about the best value lunch special in the city, three combos of soup, main (curry, cashew or Phad Thai) and spring rolls for a single-digit price. I'm partial to the curry, but for dinner, it's Gai

Phad Khing all the way (lots of fresh ginger, chicken, peppers, onions and black mushrooms). Bruce spends more time roaming the menu, but I notice the Gra Pau Seafood dish (squid, prawns and fish sautéed with onions, peppers, basil leaves and chillies) across the table from me pretty often.

Ron makes the rounds—clearing a plate here, delivering a drink there, always with a minute to chat—and he's organized live guitar music for the weekends. See, there's more to his end of the partnership than personality and the good sense to know a man's place.

Orathai and Ron Yamada at
Siam Orchid in Kelowna.

Minstrel Café

4638 Lakeshore Road, Kelowna
250.764.2301

I'm completely stuck on the portobello pinwheel appetizer at the Minstrel Café. Portobello mushroom, tomato salsa, goat feta cheese and mozzarella rolled and baked in a sun-dried tomato tortilla. My man never misses the fresh mussels: green curry coconut cream simmered with carrot, scallion, cilantro and those tasty little mollusks. We select a wine from the serious list and after that anything goes. We sometimes delve into the main menu with options ranging from lamb shank to roast duck, butter poached halibut to jerk chicken. Sometimes we just go with another round of tapas and knosh until the music starts. We try to arrive early for a good seat, although spending a summer evening on the patio under one of the biggest trees in the valley is fun too. Open for lunch, appy hour and dinner with live entertainment Thursday, Friday and Saturday.

19 Okanagan Grill & Bar

3509 Carrington Road, West Kelowna
250.768.3133

Upscale golf course casual is the best way I can describe this sports bar/ dining room. Killer view of greens, fairways, Okanagan Lake, mountains and, time it right, the sunset lighting up Mission Hill winery. Good thing it's got a huge patio, because you sure want to be outside in the summer. Indoors, the sage walls, mid-tone woods and stone fireplace are accented by wall-mounted carvings in First Nations salmon and orca motifs. Beef is a specialty and I went for the beef dip. It was really good (except for the dip, a bit salty), but when I snagged a bite of my man's pepper crusted hand-formed burger—plate envy. No kidding. This is the best hamburger I've tasted in the Okanagan and everybody will tell you, I'm a burger freak. It was awesome. Okay, enough, I know. But it really was amazing. Next time I got my very own.

Matterhorn Bakery

103-3640 Gosset Road, West Kelowna
250.768.3302

You know the thing about six degrees of separation—finding connections between people you'd never believe would be linked. Well, it can work for food as well. Consider the relationship between macaroni and cheese and wedding cake. Not the most likely candidates I'm sure you'd agree, but here's the thing. It started at lunch one day in a little bakery in West Kelowna.

The Matterhorn is a storefront with a few tables inside and a few more out on the sidewalk, a glass-fronted case containing calorie-loaded confections and a row of shelves on one wall laden with fresh-baked bread and buns—well, laden if you get there first thing in the morning. By two in the afternoon, the shelves are as empty as Sarah Palin's head.

Anyway, that first lunch I noticed mac and cheese on the blackboard menu and went for it. Brilliant. Real comfort food, creamy sauce, with just the right cheddar bite. Next time I was in for coffee with my mom. She favours sticky cinnamon buns so I joined her. Oh, yes! That led to another lunch, homemade chicken noodle soup; more coffee and a chocolate éclair oozing whipped cream; a take-home apple pie….

When it came time to pick a baker for my wedding cake, the choice was a foregone conclusion. I sat down with owner Ineke Heimlecher and we settled on traditional marzipan-topped fruitcake to wrap and distribute, plus a light mocha-mouse and white cake to cut. My guests were delirious, and they never knew that just six degrees of yummy treats separated their cake-rapture from a bowl of hearty mac and cheese.

Sapa Vietnamese Restaurant

103-2459 Main Street, West Kelowna
250.768.3888

I'm a confessed chopstick snob, taking pride in my ability to tweeze a grain of rice into my mouth with as much skill as any two-year-old Asian. However, it's tempting to abandon the sticks and go straight for the first four-tined metal object within reach when I'm confronted with a serving of Bun Thit Nuong Cha Gio. That's Vietnamese for the best darn meal you can cram into a single bowl—and I've found a terrific version here in West Kelowna at Sapa.

This lively cuisine first entered my gustatory repertoire during a sojourn in Toronto a few years ago when Bruce and I were getting better acquainted. A mom and pop hole-in-the-wall issued its siren call from the corner less than a hundred steps from our front door. I was so hooked on the crispy-chewy, hot-cold, raw-cooked combination of rice noodles, spring rolls, pork strips, lettuce, cucumber, bean sprouts and cilantro that Bruce finally had to issue a dictum. Vietnamese no more than twice a week! I still got awfully good with those chopsticks.

When Sapa opened nearby, I rejoiced. Even Bruce was happy. This sleek little eighteen-seat eatery decorated in tones of chocolate and sand, with a fat Buddha sitting on the counter, serves all the standard fare. We start with bulging, fresh summer rolls (prawns, pork and vermicelli wrapped in rice paper and served cold with peanut dipping sauce) and move directly to the main event. Sapa's version hides a surprise, replacing the cilantro in my Bun with mint leaves—brilliant. Alex, the four-year-old grandson with the cosmopolitan tastes, prefers the traditional Pho beef with beef ball soup. We're working on his chopstick technique.

Old Vines Restaurant

Quail's Gate Estate Winery
3303 Boucherie Road, West Kelowna
250.769.2500

The monumental occasion of our first anniversary prompts a call for reservations. Given the date in April, not exactly prime wine touring season, we figure a week in advance should be plenty of time to snag a window table for the sunset show—ngggggggh! Happily, our home view of sunsets over Okanagan Lake is as good as the restaurant's (which is to say—stupendous) or I'd be a little disappointed with having to look past other diners from our inside row table. Note to self: book next year's anniversary dinner ... now.

Everything else about the evening is stellar—including the night sky view that materializes over the course of our three-hour dinner. Given the obvious popularity of the place, I wouldn't have been surprised if our server, Mauricio Mariscal, hustled us along with some of those not-so-subtle signals beloved of haughty waiters (not him) to convey an unmistakable message of "Move it!"

But when we order Dungeness crab cake appies and a half-litre of Quail's Gate's 2009 dry Riesling, there's no "gentle" hint that now would be a good time to pick the mains. We dawdle over the crispy cakes with tart remoulade sauce, fennel and celery/apple slaw and when the carafe is running low, get around to deciding on the next course. Through the rest of the meal Mauricio and Adriana Moreno-Vogt (who we later discovered is the service manager) dance a perfectly choreographed duet around our table. Food and wine is delivered with the natural smiles and easy chat of professionals with nothing to prove.

I often opt for the day's special and this one makes me very happy—smoked chicken breast and wing drum (free range—so presumably the most contented of barnyard birds) nesting on a corn cake, newborn asparagus spears and the ingredient that clinches my choice—a bed of brilliant green curls—fresh fiddleheads. I love chefs like Roger Sleiman who come up with these little surprises.

Bruce, on the other hand, is a seafood man. When I see bouillabaisse on the menu, there's no doubt about where he's going. Dungeness crab legs, local fish, Cortez Island mussels and clams in a tomato and fennel broth with rouille and grilled crostini. He sets us up with the winery's 2008 Chardonnay and we're both in heaven—well, almost.

It's the crème caramel with a hint of maple syrup in the brittle candied lid (mine, all mine), paired with Optima dessert wine, and something involving chocolate, chocolate, chocolate, delivered to him with a complimentary anniversary taste of Quail's Gate's Tawny (port), that finally beams us through the pearly gates.

Herbs fresh from the Old Vines garden, Quail's Gate Estate Winery, West Keowna.

The Pepper Pot Grill

1822 Byland Road, West Kelowna
250.769.6383

For me, "greasy spoon" is a term of endearment. During my life in Toronto, the corner greasy—a mom and pop hole-in-the-wall with steamy windows, Formica tabletops and ketchup-splattered tri-fold menus—represented the ultimate in comfort dining. My addiction began in the hungry university years with a platter of scrambled eggs, three strips of fat-streaked bacon, two slices of thickly buttered white toast and a small mountain range of crusty-sided home fries (cholesterol afloat in a sea of grease), bottomless coffee on the side—$1.99 plus tip. I remained a regular. Leaving the greasy was one of the most heart-wrenching (o-o-h) features of my move west.

You can feel the love in my words, so you know that when I refer to the Pepper Pot Grill as a greasy spoon, I'm paying this little highway eatery a very high compliment in my dietary vocabulary. Here I find the same wonderful breakfast food, although these days I order the toast whole wheat (you can't get too much fibre) and I suspect the cook of using margarine instead of butter, but the essential ingredients remain. Naturally, the price tag isn't mired in the 1970s, but you can still eat the daily breakfast special for under five bucks.

The only problem with the Pepper Pot is getting a seat. In spite of serious expansion (they knocked down a wall and invaded the shop next door), it's still as good as winning the lottery to snag a table. The place just opens for breakfast and lunch and you'd think it was the only restaurant west of the bridge—especially Sunday mornings. Bruce and I have to carefully time our arrival between church crowds—early and late services. Misjudge by as little as five minutes and its standing room only. Seriously, they should take reservations. When nothing but comfort food will do.

Aegean Grill

5818 Beach Avenue, Peachland
250.707.1177

Family restaurants rock. I'm talking family-run establishments where your server has a personal stake in whether or not you have a good time—and you know that the pot-jockey behind the stove is turning out dishes straight from mama-granny-auntie's recipe box. My personal favourites are small, ethnic restaurants—the kind of corner eateries you find in big-city neighbourhoods whose entire clientele lives within a five-block radius. Imagine my joy when I found just such a place in downtown West Kelowna. Imagine my chagrin when it recently moved farther away to Peachland.

The Aegean Grill has all the ingredients—storefront location (now on the busy Peachland waterfront); meet-n-greet by co-owner Amber Russell—who also takes orders and serves the food (caring very much whether or not you have a good time); water topped by next-generation server-in-training, Tyler (who charms everybody with her smile); and master of the kitchen, Sean Russell (whose mother, happily, was Greek and possessed a terrific recipe box).

This is not a fast-food establishment. Sean's back there making every homemade dish: chewy kalamari rings; grape-leaf dolmates with a thick, lemony sauce; spanakopita wrapped in filo pastry the colour of parchment—its flaky layers thin as sheets of writing paper; creamy tzatziki for dipping—abundantly flecked with dill … and I'm still on the appetizer platter. He does all the standards like souvlaki and roast lamb with the required sides of salad, rice and roast potatoes (Greek food is so over the top), but my undisputed favourite is his baby lamb chops. This dish is always a bit of a mental minefield for me. I just have to banish the image of cuddly little critters and focus on the tenderness and flavour of the two-bite medallions. Bottom line, I am a carnivore. Wrap this meal with Sean's own cake-custard-almond-whipped-cream Ek Mek. That's all she wrote.

Gasthaus on the Lake

5790 Beach Avenue, Peachland
250.767.6625

When my mom hit the big eight-O, we needed a celebration fit for a royal lady—never mind that all the guests wanted to eat their brains out and revel like a bunch of rowdy peasants. Imagine my relief when I found a place in Peachland that let us do it all. Everybody knows the Gasthaus—splendiferous patio, fab views (the lake, passing minis, and I'm not talking cars here), best schnitzel sandwich this side of Bavaria.

But you may not know that the Gasthaus also hosts a Medieval Feast—complete with livery, lord and lady coronets and one jester's hat per table. My son-in-law donned ours, no questions asked. (He's a team player—or a realist—no judgement on my part.) He certainly made no joke of the feast. Man, that guy can eat! And this is the place for it. A huge cauldron of homemade soup warmed in the walk-in fireplace is served with big rounds of bread. The main courses arrive all together in a cast-iron pan so huge it takes chef Devin Smith or chef Werner Fischer plus another burly helper to carry it into the dining room.

This is no meal for the anti-carnivorous. Any vegetarian not traumatized by the huge boar's head on the table (topped by one wag in our group with an Indiana Jones fedora) would surely faint dead away at the extravagance of chops, bratwurst, duck, ribs and schnitzel piled alongside huge mounds of rice, roast potatoes, red cabbage, sauerkraut and on and on. Wine and beer flow to taste and by some freak of nature, some people can even cram in dessert, at least my son-in-law did. Bottom line, this feast made one eighty-year-old lady and nine gluttonous peasants, very happy.

Medieval feast at Gasthaus
on the Lake, Peachland.

Gasthaus on the Lake, Peachland.

Two chefs, Debbie Slade and Tom Cornwall, in their kitchen at Two Chefs restaurant in Peachland.

Quick break.

Two Chefs

6575 Hwy 97, South, Peachland
250.767.1991

It's a long way to Tipperary, but not so far to the Two Chefs. And if you manage to squeeze in on English pub night (Saturdays, twice a month), you'll be singing all the tunes from Great War ditties to *Henry the Eighth—I am, I am*. Even if you can't claim a drop of British blood, Tom Cornwall's Union Jack Tie (matching thirty-five mini flags strung from the beams and tacked to the walls, I counted), royal family photos from good Queen Vicki to our own Queen Liz, horse brasses, beer mats and chunky trestle tables imbedded with coinage of the realm—will.

This place is all about good company and really good, home-cooked food. Tom, a retired British army VIP chef, and Debbie Slade got together while working on an Alberta military base. It took them two years to find the right location for their culinary duet, a little truck stop on Highway 97 at the big bend in Okanagan Lake. Debbie definitely claims the best kitchen view in the valley and it's just as good from the restaurant and patio.

Take your chances at lunch, but make reservations for dinner. Always bring an appetite for pure comfort food: roast pork with stuffing, shepherd's pie; sausage and mash; spinach, leek and brie pie; fish and chips. The chips are fresh-cut and Debbie personally peels the potatoes for the mash. She also makes all the pastries from scratch (zero trans fats—no comment on the calories), like deep-dish Okanagan apple pie smothered in creamy, yellow custard (sigh) and Cornish pasties.

The steak and kidney pie is Tom's domain and he handles all the front-of-house duties. Sundays he deals out plate loads of roast beef piled on mashed potatoes, with unEnglish munchy veg and roast potatoes, topped by a meaty/crispy/airy Yorkshire pudding and about a gallon of pan-dripping gravy. You'll want a beer to offset the sinus-sizzling horseradish (optional).

Victoria Rd Deli & Bistro

108-13615 Victoria Road, North, Summerland
250.583.9343

While chefs all over the Okanagan talk about fresh local ingredients, Roger Gillespie really walks the walk. Like many good eateries, Victoria Rd's menu changes often, though you can always count on specialties like handmade smoked duck ham and fresh corned beef. Being a fry fan, I was knocked out by Roger's signature mixed frites—yams, potatoes and parsnips (of all things)—and then I discovered I was dipping these little tasties into his signature smoked tomato and cherry ketchup made with heirloom tomatoes grown on his own property. Sensational.

The smart twenty-seat dining space incorporates a trendy concrete bar where you can sit and watch the action in the open kitchen. Stop by the bistro's alter ego where the deli selection covers all the essentials for a wine country al fresco lunch or take home dinner. Features include Okanagan Street Food pasta and sauces, Vij's Indian cuisine, Poplar Grove and Gort's Gouda cheeses, deli meats and bottled condiments from lots of Okanagan producers.

Chef Roger Gillespie even makes his own ketchup at Victoria Rd Deli & Bistro in Summeland.

Dream Café

67 Front Street, Penticton
250.490.9012

Visually delicious. The paprika and milk chocolate walls, oriental rugs, wicker chairs and pillow-piled benches give the Dream Café a decidedly eastern flavour. Not sure where the mounted buffalo head fits in, but it works. So do the long-tail dragon kites flying high across the ceiling and the walls lined with photos of musicians who play there. It's dim and casual inside and outside the shady patio is a great place for people watching on Colourful Front Street.

Pierre Couture likes to mix it up on the menu with a multi-ethnic selection that visits Mexico with huevos rancheros, and Europe, the Middle East and Thailand with Black Forest ham, falafel and humus, and mango roasted vegetable wraps. He scoots around the globe for a taste of Asia in the tandoori chicken then zips back home for wild salmon and beef tenderloin. Whew, I'm exhausted.

Showtime on entertainment nights is 8 p.m. and the table is yours from 6 p.m. on. The musical line-up is as eclectic as the menu and with name artists like Murray McLaughlan on stage, shows often sell out.

Eclectic menu to match eclectic music at Penticton's Dream Café.

Theo's Restaurant

687 Main Street, Penticton
250.492.4019

When *My Big Fat Greek Wedding* hit the screen, the Portokalos family showed us Greek family values: "marry a Greek boy, have Greek babies and feed everyone." The first two didn't exactly work out—but man, did everybody eat.

Penticton's Theodosakis family shares this fundamental preoccupation and indulges it with everybody who dines at Theo's. "It's not just a restaurant, it's food, it's stories, it's life," says Mary, who helped her husband Theo open the eatery more than thirty years ago. The couple, both from Crete though they met here in Canada, likely caused some turned up noses when they introduced Greek staples like squid to meat-and-potatoes Okanaganites. But their recipe for hospitality and great home cooking soon won over the locals and their son Nikos continues the tradition (along with starting a few of his own—but that's another story).

Passing through the modest front door on Main Street is like stepping through a stargate to a sunny Mediterranean island. Beyond the dim and cosy front rooms you emerge into an atrium filled with light and trees and flowers. All around are family mementos, images captured by Nikos' lens and recorded for others to share—a photo of Mary's father and his beloved Penticton almond tree, cousins Nikos met on his first boyhood trip to Crete, Mary and Theo through the years and his own two daughters. It feels like a family home and you're a welcome guest. So bring on the food!

I never know where to start (or stop). A plate of salty Kalamata olives; taramasalata (mushed up fish roe dip, sounds yucky … tastes yummy. I could eat buckets. Wait, I do eat buckets); whole wheat pita to scoop up the creamiest tzatziki; and paithakia—tiny, perfect lamb chops (forget cute-and-cuddly … just enjoy). Match it up with one of the best selections of Okanagan wines in the valley and if you've still got room for dessert, you can handle a Greek wedding.

Nikos, Mary and Theo Theodosakis in the atrium at Theo's in Penticton.

Lost Moose Lodge

2301 Beaverdell Road, Penticton
250.490.0526

Neither snow, nor rain, nor heat, nor gloom of night stays this chef from his appointed grill … Okay, so I've taken a few liberties with the quote—but you get the drift. And everybody who's found the Lost Moose Lodge knows what I'm talking about—Phil Basil, armed with long-handled flipper and tongs, manning his outdoor barbe, year-round. The man deserves a medal.

It's a flavour you can't duplicate, fresh air seared right into the food. And unlike some backyard chefs I could name, Phil provides no gratuitous charcoal, just beautifully cooked steak, ribs, chicken and burgers (for carnivores and veg-heads). Reason enough to drive ten kilometres up a mountain road. I mean, who would go all that way just for the view—Apex, the Cathedral Rim and the Cascades, snow tipped most of the year; Penticton laid out in the valley more than a thousand metres below; eagles sailing in lazy circles; great arcing rainbows.

Although you might make the trip for the novelty of eating in a restaurant constructed mainly of timber recycled from the 1994 Garnet fire. And I can't think of a single other eatery where the entertainment includes watching a KVR model train chug around the tree-trunk-beamed ceiling and counting the rings on your table. I'm not talking wet glass marks here. These tables are sliced from the same gigantic ponderosa that was split to make the bar. And figuring out the age of this tragically fallen hero is a great way to pass the time between courses. I singled out one hundred and twenty rings, but Phil's wife and partner, Kathy, assures me that the official count is one hundred and twenty-eight—some of those years were pretty thin.

But there's nothing sparse about the menu and if you plan to overindulge/overimbibe and don't want to hazard the downbound switchbacks and the possibility of finding the lost moose with your front bumper, reservations for a night in one of the lodge's cabins could be considered an investment in a bright future.

Cobblestone Wine Bar & Restaurant

3625 1st Street, Naramata
250.496.6808

If you're going to run a wine bar, you couldn't pick a much better spot than the heart of the Naramata Bench. Bonus if you can operate out of one of the Okanagan's most venerable historic sites, the meticulously restored Naramata Heritage Inn & Spa. Cobblestone scores on all points. I personally prefer the intimate surroundings, subterranean warmth and subdued lighting of the cellar venue, but there's also no denying the appeal of its secluded, leafy patio.

Originally designed to showcase BC wine to guests of the inn, visitors to the valley and locals, the main focus is on the Naramata Bench terroir with an extensive selection of other Okanagan wines. During the high season, you'll find a selection of wines available by the glass along with a staff that's ready, willing and able to help with pairing suggestions.

Chef Thomas Render likes to highlight sustainable and environmentally friendly meats, seafood and artisan products, changing his menu to reflect what's in season and using the inn's garden to supply herbs and produce. His West Coast paella is a great combination of flavours and the braised short rib is an ongoing best seller. But I never manage to get past his brilliant "small plates"—organic carrot and ginger soup; asparagus, fingerling potato and warm goat cheese salad; and rock oven fired hearth bread with a choice of accompaniments like Poplar Grove cheeses, artichoke and olive tapenade, artisan chorizo and duck rillette. Cobblestone even lays on live music Friday nights.

Best of India

36094 97th Street, Oliver
250.498.0872

We're frustrated. This is our third trek to Oliver for Indian food and every time we come up empty (pun intended). We always mismanage our time and arrive between meal hours (less dawdling at wineries, perhaps). Regardless, it's three in the afternoon, the sun is blazing and the door is locked. "I can't believe we've done it again," I rail—possibly a bit over loudly. As we retreat around the corner to where the car is parked, Bruce suggests an alternative. I'm not in the mood. A voice from above intervenes (something cosmic?).

"Can you come back in fifteen minutes," it asks. We look up. Perched high on a ladder a bearded man in a green turban smiles down at us. "Absolutely," we reply. "I will meet you then," he says. (Definitely cosmic.)

Despair turns to joy and soon my taste buds are singing. True to his word, a quarter hour later, Jaswinder Sidhu is unlocking the door and ushering us to a table in the large dining room with its inviting cayenne, chocolate and lime walls, elephant motifs and brightly striped tablecloths. The wait time at normal meal hours in summer can be long, but here we are alone and pampered. His wife brings the menus and we go straight for our regulars: samosa starters, butter chicken (I can't help it, I love this stuff), aloo Gobi—cauliflower and baked potatoes cooked in curry sauce—and for Bruce, because he can take it, Saag lamb. Not being overwhelmed with other patrons, Jaswinder has time to talk.

While I scoop the rich buttery/tomato sauce with a strip of fresh, warm naan, he confirms what I've heard. In a former life (well, actually this life, but the part he spent in India) Jaswinder was a machinist and homeopath. Lack of work in his trade caused him to abandon his machine tools and open a restaurant, but he still uses his homeopathic skills in the kitchen, selecting spices that work for the body. He says this food doesn't taste just like what you find in India because he's adapted the flavours to suit Canadian tastes. I'll say—and talk about service above and beyond!

Passa Tempo

1200 Rancher Creek Road, Osoyoos
250.495.8007

My first experience with Passa Tempo, the chic bistro at Spirit Ridge
Vineyard Resort & Spa, was a dinner I won't forget. It was my amazing good fortune to be seated at the restaurant's twenty-person alder
wood table next to wine guru John Schreiner. He patiently talked me
through a succession of wonderful Okanagan vintages, representing
a good number of the more than one hundred and forty labels on the
wine list from the valley and beyond, that were paired with a succession of equally wonderful dishes (and he did it without making me feel
like a complete wine dolt).

With the food I was on much more solid ground. I suffer no inferiority complex when it comes to appreciating the finer points of West
Coast mussels and daily terrines, pan seared Queen Charlotte halibut
or grilled bison ribeye. Jeremy Luypen, a former basketball jock who
found joy in the kitchen and took his initial training at Okanagan College, has donned the tall hat as executive chef and promises a locally inspired menu that will feature a daily rolling seven-course Chef's
Table tasting menu paired with wine.

View from the patio at Passa
Tempo includes vineyards, desert,
mountains and Osoyoos Lake.

Subject Index

Acknowledgements

PUBLISHING THIS BOOK has been a truly collaborative effort. If you've read all the way through, you know that I have to start my list of acknowledgements with the two guys who take such a beating in my stories. Bruce Kemp, who shamelessly encourages my love of food, tries to teach me about wine, willingly shares his vast experience as writer and photographer and also shares my life; Jim White, octogenarian mountain goat, intrepid hiking partner, advisor, proof reader and the life-long learner who taught himself Illustrator so he could draw the maps for this book—to both of you, my heartfelt thanks. Thanks also to my daughter Brandie, my biggest fan and the fine person who (with a little help from her good hubby) gave me the book title by making me a grandma. On the technical side, thanks to Mishell Raedeke for her imaginative cover design and for cajoling me into going full colour to make the most of her interior design; to Karen Slivar, proof reader extraordinaire, for her invaluable work on the editing; and to all the people at Friesens for their patience and guidance through the printing process.

Photo credits:
All photos are by Laurie Carter except as follows:
Bruce Kemp: p. 248, p. 250, P. 259 (top), p. 260, p. 265
James White: p.28
Roseanne Van Ee: p. 59
John Kirbyson: p. 81

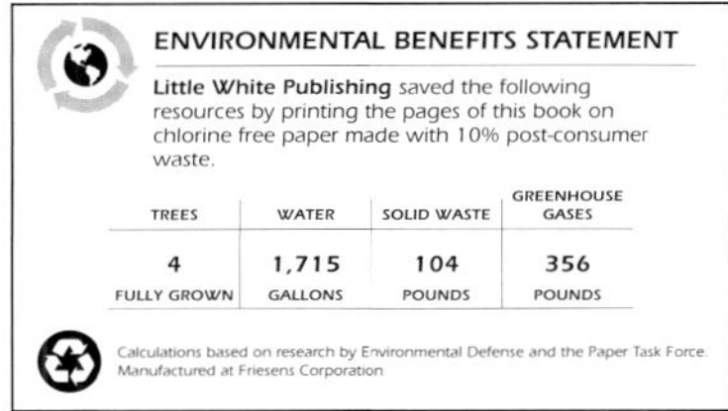

TREES	WATER	SOLID WASTE	GREENHOUSE GASES
4	1,715	104	356
FULLY GROWN	GALLONS	POUNDS	POUNDS

Author Biography

LAURIE CARTER IS AN AWARD-WINNING writer and photographer whose work appears in newspapers, magazines and online. Originally from Ontario, she has lived in the Okanagan Valley since 1991. Carter shares a cozy home with her husband and two SPCA rescue cats, and waits impatiently for her grandson's next visit.

www.LaurieCarter.com